# AMERICAN VALUES PROJECTED ABROAD

## A SERIES FUNDED BY THE EXXON EDUCATION FOUNDATION

Vol. I   Western Heritage And American Values:
Law, Theology And History
By
Alberto Coll

Vol. II   Political Traditions And Contemporary Problems
Edited by
Kenneth W. Thompson

Vol. III   Institutions and Values in World Affairs
Edited by
Kenneth W. Thompson

Copyright © 1982 by

**University Press of America, Inc.**

P.O. Box 19101, Washington, D.C. 20036

Printed in the United States of America

ISBN (Perfect): 0-8191-2589-X
ISBN   (Cloth): 0-8191-2588-1

Library of Congress Catalog Card Number: 82-40160

# POLITICAL TRADITIONS AND CONTEMPORARY PROBLEMS

## VOL II

### EDITED BY
### KENNETH W. THOMPSON

*THE CONTRIBUTORS
TO
THIS VOLUME
GRATEFULLY DEDICATE
IT TO
MRS. SHIRLEY KINGSBURY
OUR MOST REMARKABLE
SECRETARY*

# TABLE OF CONTENTS

# PREFACE

The aim of the present volume is to help the student and citizen understand the historic and philosophical sources of American political values and their manifestation in the United States' role in the world. That role has been and continues to be played out as a mission, the subject of the first essay by an outstanding young international relations theorist, Brian E. Klunk. For the founders of the republic, the American mission was best served by the image of America as "a city on a hill" or "a beacon of liberty." For some moderns, the spread of liberty requires interventionist actions around the world in part because political rivals are themselves intervening everywhere. Whatever one's idea of mission, it is vital to understand the religious, philosophical and political basis of the concept. The author of the first chapter of the book has undertaken this task.

Daniel G. Lang is a political philosopher who seeks to relate Greek political thought and Judeo-Christian thought. He has analyzed the relationship of Augustine and Aquinas to Niebuhr and John Courtney Murray in earlier writings. In the present eassay, he traces the connections between Christian and classical political thought as they have shaped American political ideas.

Alan Pino is a classical political philosopher who seeks to evaluate the differences between "the ancients and the moderns." He points to the break in political thinking which occurs in the writings of Machiavelli and Hobbes and leads to a shift in ideas regarding the effect of man's relations to political society. For Pino, the search for virtue and fulfillment is replaced by the quest for self-preservation and security in the moderns. Consistent with but addressed more explicitly to American political values is a discussion of Locke and modern political thought by Dr. Robert A. Strong. In his earlier research and writing, Dr. Strong has been concerned with the historic problem, obscured by some contemporary political scientists, of the interaction of statesmanship and bureaucratic politics. I try to sum up the importance of the elements of convergence and contradiction between the three strains of political philosophy that are the historic foundations of both American political thought and American foreign policy.

The second broad area discussed in the volume, the first having been the sources of American political values, is the effect on contemporary problems of the nature of American values. What influence if any do historic political ideas have on the way Americans confront such urgent issues as violence, political ethics by congressmen and senators and human rights. Professor Dante Germino, the University of Virginia's most distinguished political philosopher, and I jointly discuss these questions.

The clash and mutual reinforcement of the several political traditions influencing current political thought can also be seen in postwar attempts to formulate American foreign policy. David Clinton is the author of a forthcoming book which reexamines the concept of the national interest viewed in the context of postwar problems in American foreign policy such as the Marshall Plan, China policy and human rights. His essay foreshadows a more extensive discussion in his important major treatise.

Having considered the various political philosophers on which American political thought is based and their implications for contemporary problems, I undertake to discuss "limits and possibilities" for relating theory and practice in a concluding note.

Two of the country's ablest and most thoughtful foundation leaders, while in no way responsible for the contents of this volume, have in fact made it possible. President Robert L. Payton and Dr. Leon Bramson of the Exxon Education Foundation not only helped us by providing material assistance but inspired some of the thinking on which the volume is based. We are exceedingly grateful to them and to the Foundation. Their encouragement of our work both with funds and ideas exemplifies what that remarkable American social invention, the American foundation, is capable of doing. They exemplify for us the workings of present day philanthropy at its best.

# I. THE VISION OF AMERICA AND THE WORLD

## CHAPTER ONE
## THE AMERICAN MISSION
### Brian E. Klunk

I have always believed that this land was placed here between two great oceans by some divine plan. It was placed here by a special kind of people—people who had the courage to uproot themselves and leave hearth and homeland and come to what in the beginning was the most undeveloped wilderness possible. . . . And our destiny and that destiny can build a land that will be for all mankind a shining city on a hill.

> Ronald W. Reagan
> 21 September 1980
> Debate with John Anderson

President Reagan (as did his predecessor Jimmy Carter) has tried to evoke the sense and spirit of the American mission. The belief that America has a special destiny or mission has been a recurrent element in the tradition of American political ideas. The concept of mission has been a powerful notion of the purpose of the United States in its relations with the rest of the world. The idea of the American mission is that the United States has been *chosen* to accomplish an important task—perfecting the values and institutions of republican democracy and somehow transmitting the values and institutions of free government to other nations. A sense of mission existed during the American colonial period and at the founding of the Republic; that sense persisted throughout the nineteenth century and became a sentiment of importance for the whole world as

1-1

the United States emerged as a great power in 1898 and a super-power after World War II. Perhaps only the disillusionment which accompanied the dual trauma of the past fifteen years—Vietnam and Watergate—has seriously diminished the popular sense that we Americans are a unique people with a message for the rest of the world and a duty to spread that message.

The United States is not altogether exceptional in its sense of mission. Perhaps most states have maintained, at one time or another, a sentiment of grandeur, singularity, and purpose. In his funeral oration, Pericles spoke of Athenian institutions as a model for other city-states and Athens itself as an education for Greece. Imperial Britain steadfastly shouldered the "White Man's Burden" and administered the empire upon which the sun never set. A common theme of the rhetoric of the spokesmen of the states of the so-called Third World during the 1950s and 1960s was that their emergence into a system of international relations plagued by Soviet-American rivalry would bring about a moral rejuvenation and pacification of world politics. Though extremely weak, these states claimed that their example of non-alignment in the Cold War would, in effect, save the superpowers from themselves.

None of these visions persisted. Before the end of the Peloponnesian Wars, the Athenians, according to Thucydides, set aside the noble-sounding pronouncements of Pericles for the harsh cynicism of the Melian Dialogue. "The strong do what they have the power to do and the weak accept what they have to accept." After the 1956 Suez debacle, the British found their "burden" quickly lifted as most of the remnants of the empire gained independence. And according to many commentators, the proud spirit of purpose displayed by imperial Britain has dissipated for one reason or another. As for the mission of the Third World, those states have been forced to meet the exigencies of survival. Moral rejuvenation has not been wrought by states plagued by poverty, overpopulation, starvation, political instability, a variety of wars, and an assortment of unsavory personalities such as Idi Amin and the Emperor Bokassa.

Missions, or rather the sense of them, are often fleeting. Young nations, dynamic empires, states "on-the-make" almost seem to assume their special purpose and destiny. To have a sense of mission is to look forward with optimism and more than a little self-satisfaction to futures of growth, expansion, and influence. Americans have been an exceptional people in this regard. Our history has been, for the most part, a chronicle of almost uninterrupted growth, prosperity, expansion, and increasing power. Even in the current period of economic stagflation, strong commercial competition from Japan and Western Europe, and frustrated political power abroad, the results of opinion surveys indicate that most Americans believe that the future will be better, at least for themselves and their families.

The question should be raised, however, whether the spirit and sense of mission persists in America today. Can a nation be said to have a sense of mission if feelings of personal optimism do not extend to society as a whole? Does post-industrial America still foster a sentiment of having a transforming work to perform in the world? Both Presidents Carter and Reagan have tried to evoke that sense through their public statements and, to an extent, through their policies. Still, some doubt the existence of a continued popular sense of the American mission.[1]

This essay is a preliminary and cursory investigation into the meaning and sources of the idea and sense of the American mission. The nature of the concept of mission, the philosophical and religious roots of that concept will be discussed, and a few comments will be made about the importance of the idea of mission for American foreign policy. It is to be hoped that such a preliminary discussion will make possible more detailed and exhaustive studies of the contribution of the idea and sense of the American mission to particular approaches to foreign relations.

*Unique Origins.* The idea of mission has two essential elements. The first is that a nation has an exceptional, in the sense of being unique, origin. The second is that the same nation has been selected to perform a particular duty. The two elements are inextricably linked. Any of a number of groups may select its own purpose. The notion of mission, on the other hand, implies a sense of inevitability—of having been ordered by a greater power to accomplish some end. If a nation believes that it has a mission, it must also believe that it has been singled out or chosen—that it is exceptional in its origins.

The history of the United States, perhaps more than that of any other country, fosters a sense of particular origin. American history has a beginning, a definite and accessible beginning. We know the men and women who started our country. We know when they arrived on this continent, when they started towns, when they established churches, built schools, and created their political institutions. Though we have romanticized our founders, we still can recognize them. It is possible to visit the Monticellos and Mount Vernons and walk through the gardens and homes of the people who began the United States. America was created at a definite point in history. A new country was established in a land where none had existed before. A new nation was created on a continent that was seemingly untouched.

The sense of "createdness" is quite conducive to a spirit of mission. The founding of a new state where none had existed before allows its citizens to think of themselves as a departure from the flow of history. If a nation is to be the agent for the moral regeneration of the world, that nation should not be tainted by the sins of the past nor limited by the many ties of traditional practice. In much the same way that many fundamentalist Christians find it incompatible with their faith to view mankind as part of an evolutionary biological process and insist that man is the product of a discrete act of creation, those who believe in the mission of their nation are supported by the belief that their nation was similarly created.

Not only was America created, it was created in a country of magnificent breadth, grandeur, and potential. Early Americans could hardly be faulted for thinking that they had found in such a land a New Canaan. That such an incredible country should have been left undiscovered by "civilized" people for so long has led men to posit that the North American continent was preserved—held in waiting—for the creation of the United States.

The striking continuity of American history has lent added potency to notions of createdness and singularity. We make much in our Fourth-of-July speeches of the fact that ours is the longest surviving constitutional republic in the world. There are no violent breaks in our history—no revolutions or coups d'etat. Our "revolution" was not a revolution so much as an act of preservation of the "rights of Englishmen." Perhaps the only political innovation derived from the American Revolution is federalism. Even the horror of the Civil War is venerated as a national crucible testing the probity of our purpose and the integrity of our institutions. American history books honor the memory of the leaders of the rebellion as valiant, principled men. And hundreds have made a hobby of the recreation and reenactment of what were at the time some of the most brutal battles in history. Nothing stands between us and our beginnings. We continue to live our history. Perhaps this is why Americans are often so little interested in the study of history.

Thus the United States is better suited than almost any other state (with the obvious exception of Israel) to maintain a commitment to a sense of mission. The basic facts of American history—the creation of a new nation in a well-preserved and abundant land of great and varied natural resources and the relatively unbroken stream of American history—are unusual when compared to the experience of other states and are exactly those conditions which are most congenial to a sustained popular sense of mission.

*The Myth of the Americans.* Complementing the notion of unique origins is the notion that the American people are exceptional in all manner of virtues. Independence, industry, pragmatism, and generosity all are characteristics which traditionally have been attributed to the American people. Many early Americans felt that they had left behind a Europe which was sordid and corrupt, fraught with impiety and depravity. European society was widely thought to be decadent and European manners frivolous. In America, people would not be tainted by the influence of Old World habits.

Two types stand out as models of the virtuous American: the farmer and the pioneer. The American farmer has been lionized by social philosophers like Thomas Jefferson and captured as the embodiment of solid, if somewhat grim, American morality in Grant Wood's *American Gothic.* The farmer was at once neither tainted by too much of decadent European civilization nor made savage by unruly nature. His work was made noble by his status as a free man and his participation in the work of creation. It was the farmer who brought the order of the garden out of the seeming chaos of the forest.[2] The farmer personified the best aspects of the American character as he worked hard, usually alone or with only his family's help, and depended on the success of his own efforts for his prosperity.

The experience of settling the western frontier has been widely credited with forging the particular nature of the American character, and the pioneer is another personification of the special virtues of the American people. The farmer was hardworking and independent; the pioneer was courageous, resourceful, able to endure and eager to seek the challenges of nature. The farmer established himself in the wilderness and made it bloom, but the pioneer pushed against a powerful frontier and made it move. The farmer tended the new land; the pioneer extended it. The frontier West and its availability for conquest linked notions of grandeur and power to notions of godliness and innocence.[3]

New men in a new land could hardly resist the temptation to believe that their novelty meant that they had been chosen to perform a great task. Although we copied our political institutions and theory from Europe, we Americans came to believe that our freedom from Old World corruption and the bracing nature of American life made America singularly able to preserve and perfect not only moral but political and social virtue in the form of the westward looking republic.

*America and the Kingdom of God.* The notion of the American mission is a complex one which has many roots. One root which should not be ignored is the religious one—the idea that God created this land and preserved it for the American people and the United States so that we could fulfill some great purpose of His. Religious fundamentalism has long had a powerful influence on American thought and values. So, the impact of religious ideas, particularly the idea that the United States was created to carry out some divine plan, on the notion of the American mission must be considered in the context of this discussion.[4]

The theological tradition of the Puritans is frequently identified as one of the principle roots of the sense and idea of the American mission. Many of the elements discussed above have come to us from the Puritan experience in New England: the rejection of Europe, the spirit of having started anew in an untouched land, and the feeling of being a people of special virtue.

The Puritans came to America to escape persecution and to be free to practice their chosen faith. That is true enough. They had been rejected, by and large, in Europe, but the rejection was more than mutual. The Reformation had been frustrated in Europe, they thought, largely through the machinations of the most unreconstructed and diabolical operatives of the Roman Church—the Society of Jesus. The pilgrimage to the New World was not so much a flight from danger to freedom as an attack on the Old World's immorality and inability to perfect the Christian religion.

By carrying the fight to New England, the Puritans free from European corruption hoped to be able to determine whether it was possible to create *de novo* a community where men would live according to God's will. John Winthrop, for example, intended to create a Christianized state founded upon Christian principles and led by upright Christian men.[5] Such a blessed community would be a "city on a hill" providing an example of moral rectitude and civic virtue for Europe.

From this notion of the "city on a hill" is derived the similar but more political concept of "liberty enlightening the world." One aspect of the tradition of the American mission is the conviction that by maintaining and perfecting our political institutions and principles, we Americans would set a sparkling and irresistible example which would lead all people everywhere to long for our blessings and advantages and eventually to adopt our values and institutions.

The religious roots of the idea of the American mission should be explored further. A deeper appreciation of the complexity and pervasiveness of the idea of the American mission comes from a consideration of the importance of the apocalyptic view of history which can be found in American Christian, especially fundamentalist Protestant, thought. This tradition of thought which continues to appeal to many[6] holds that the United States occupies a crucial place in God's design for the world.

One of the great innovations of the Reformation was the renewed emphasis given to the Bible as the immediate source of information about God, the relationship of God with mankind, and God's plan for history. The Protestant rediscovery, so to speak, of the Bible led to a new interest in the idea of continuity in the history of salvation. That history proceeded in an unbroken line from Abraham and Moses to Jesus Christ and the Christian Church. If the history chronicled in the Bible is to be taken literally, if the whole of the bible is to be considered as revealed and absolute truth, then the prophesies of the Old Testament Book of Daniel and the New Testament Book of Revelation must be considered predictions of the rise and fall of nations and the course of the history of the world.

The Book of Revelation contains a prophesy of a series of struggles between the forces of Christ and the servants of the anti-Christ lasting until the end of the world. The penultimate conflict between these two camps, according to the Biblical prophesy, is the battle of Armageddon in which the anti-Christ is defeated and after which the millennium, a period of 1000 years during which holiness is to prevail and the reign of God is to exist on the earth, is begun.

Ernest Lee Tuveson, whose book *Redeemer Nation: The Idea of America's Millenial Role* is perhaps the only scholarly explication of the importance of the apocalyptic view of history in American thought, observes the crucial transition over  time from the Augustinian concept of the ''City of God'' which must coexist until the end of time with the sinful ''City of Man'' to the idea that in accordance with God's law a chosen nation could and would bring about the kingdom of God on earth.[7] The original chosen nation, of course, was the nation of Israel but, according to the American apocalyptic view, the United States, the inheritor of the Anglo-Saxon Protestant tradition, became the New Zion and the new agent of God's historical plan.

The belief that salvation is a product of a historical process and that a single nation can be chosen as the agent of that process is at once an optimistic notion and a violent vision. It is an optimistic view because history becomes a story of movement toward ultimate perfection. A subscriber to this reading of history need not worry about his purpose, the meaning of his life, his place in the grand scheme of things. Existential dilemmas are resolved in a most satisfying way. The purpose of the American Christian and his nation is to prepare the way for the near-utopian millennium. On the other hand, the apocalyptic vision is one of constant warfare and implacable conflict between the forces of good and evil. Even the millennium, according to the prophesy of the Book of Revelation, is to be followed by one final, brief but decisive conflagration.

Tuveson argues that millenialist thinking has been prevalent among English-speaking protestants since the late seventeenth century, and he has noted elements of an apocalyptic reading of history in the writing of many early Americans, including influential figures such as John Adams,[8] literary figures like Mark Twain, and many other authors, social observers, and politicians.

Even those who are not faithful practitioners of the Christian religion may find that the way they view the world is affected by the images derived from an apocalyptic reading of history.

But as the apocalyptic way of thinking becomes divorced from the underlying theology, the movement of history through wars, slaughters, implacable conflict comes to appear simply as the iron law of nature. In every situation, for example, we must see a "confrontation: of the righteous and the wicked; the massive conflict is inevitable, and everyone must identify with his cause."

There is frequently a tendency among those who refer to the traditional concept of the American mission in their discussions of America's role in the world to argue that only the "city on a hill" notion is a true expression of the American religious tradition. Interventionist policies, they would argue, are not in keeping with this facet of the American sense of mission. They therefore deprecate American attempts actively to encourage liberal, democratic social and political developments abroad." Such arguments do not adequately take into consideration the complexity of the religious roots of the idea of the American mission. Certainly, the "city on a hill" notion of the irresistible attraction of the American example has had an enduring influence on perspectives of the purpose and role of the United States. However, the impact of apocalyptic thinking—the view of history as a series of conflicts between good and evil—has been to add the sense of America's responsibility to oppose directly forces in the world which are not in sympathy with American values and principles. These elements of the American religious tradition are not totally compatible, but they are both important and both have affected the several ways in which the notion of the American mission has been interpreted.

*Secular Roots.* It would be incorrect to suggest that the only sources of the notion of the American mission are religious. The concept of the mission is a complex one, and this complexity becomes increasingly evident to anyone studying it. In many ways, it is not one idea but a cluster of ideas which have gathered themselves under the rubric of "mission." The ideas of the Enlightenment are ostensibly secular in nature, emphasizing the possibility of continued progress based on the application of reason rather than eventual salvation for the faithful. Still, the philosophy of the Enlightenment must be considered as an important source of the tradition of the American mission of roughly equal influence with the American religious tradition. Enlightenment ideas were especially important to the founders of the American republic, men such as Benjamin Franklin, Thomas Jefferson, John Adams, and the chief propagandist of the American Revolution, Thomas Paine.

Although the philosophers of the Enlightenment were chiefly concerned with domestic politics, they also discussed international relations and were convinced that the application of reason would bring international peace to a state system plagued by wars which resulted from the egotistical, passion-driven struggle for power.

Foreign policy and its tools—diplomacy, the balance of power—were considered the corrupt elements of a system of secrecy and intrigue which could not possibly result in peace for Europe. The more radical of these thinkers argued that the horrors of the state system were tied inevitably to monarchical absolutism—only democratic or republican polities, free of the power-seeking egotism of personal rule, would be rid of the abuses of traditional foreign policy. More moderate figures thought that peace could be secured by drawing the interests of states together through increased economic transactions among states. Economic inter-dependence would replace the divisive logic of "power politics" with the unifying influence of "economic politics."

Many Americans accepted the Enlightenment criticism of the European state system. In much the same way that religious thinkers saw America as an opportunity to carry to completion the work of the Reformation, some political thinkers saw in the United States the occasion to create a political system free from the corruption of Europe, the *Novus Ordo Seclorum* declared on the Great Seal of the United States.

Thomas Paine, whose ideas flow principally from the European Enlightenment, positively despaired of the rest of the world. In his famous pamphlet *Common Sense,* he wrote, "Freedom hath been hunted around the globe. Asia and Africa have long expelled her, Europe regards her like a stranger, and England hath given her warning to depart." For the Paine of *Common Sense,* only America could begin the world again, preserve freedom and other republican virtues, and construct an order based on the dictates of reason free from the abuses of monarchical egotism.

Others, also influenced by the Enlightenment, were more sanguine about the future of Europe. In particular, they shared in the optimism of the Enlightenment and believed that especially through the example of the experiment begun by the American Revolution, a new age of progress, reason and harmony might begin.

An example of how it was thought that all of this might be brought about is the "Model Treaty" which was prepared by John Adams in 1776 to be proposed to the Court of France. The primary features of the treaty were the rejection of any political bond between the United States and France and the reliance, instead, on commercial ties marked by almost total freedom of trade. Relations between the United States and other countries, Adams and others hoped, could be based entirely on uninhibited commercial centers. There would be no alliances, no diplomacy, no secrecy, no intrigue, and no cause for war. Such enlightened principles were foreign to then prevailing European practice. The Revolutionary Americans hoped that by placing relations between France and the United States on a liberal basis, the Model Treaty might provide a guide for future diplomacy. American foreign policy based on the primacy of commerce would rejuvenate diplomatic practice because the powerful appeal of the American example and American markets would overcome the pernicious features of European politics and the European state system and hasten the advent of the longed-for period of harmony and reason.

The Enlightenment tradition complemented the tradition of religious thought in that both viewed the establishment of the United States as a chance to put the failures of Europe behind and to start again to create a more perfect order which would serve as an attractive example for the rest of the world. Both views have held that the creation of the United States is an important step in historical progress, bringing closer a happier time of harmony and justice. However, there are obvious and deep contradictions between the two traditions. The philosophy of the Enlightenment is essentially secular and posits that men and states guided by reason are fundamentally compatible. States and men pursuing an enlightened understanding of their self-interest can exist in harmony. Just the opposite is true of the American religious tradition. In that tradition, interests appear as the reflection of the essential righteousness or wickedness of a nation. There can be no harmony, only temporary truces, until the final victory of the righteous. According to this facet of American religious thought, the creation of the United States was a sign of progress not because the United States was the beginning of the rule of reason, but rather because the United States was the new embodiment of crusading virtue opposing evil. Timothy Dwight's poem "Columbia" published in a 1794 edition of *The Columbian Muse* has this apocalyptic flavor.

> Columbia, Columbia to glory arise,
> The queen of the world and the child of the skies;
> Thy reign is the last and the noblest of time,
> Most fruitful thy soil, most inviting thy clime;
> Let the crimes of the east ne'er encrimson thy name,
> Be freedom, and science, and virtue thy fame.
>
> \* \* \* \* \*
>
> As the day springs unbounded, thy splendour shall flow,
> And earth's little kingdoms before thee shall bow;
> While the ensigns of union, in triumph unfurl'd
> Hush the tumult of war, and give peace to the world.[12]

These ways, the Enlightenment and religious ways of thinking about America's role in the world could not have survived unaltered over the centuries of the American experience. Neither Enlightenment assumptions about impending progress and the harmony of interests nor the Protestant apocalyptic view of history are as actively proclaimed as they once were. In the first place, the novelty of the Puritan and the revolutionary experiences has worn off. Also, other intellectual currents (which are not fully considered here) have had their influence over time. However, both the religious and the Enlightenment traditions have had an impact on American thinking that can still be observed today. Both traditions have added to the idea that America is a particularly virtuous land with a duty to transform the world and as such help us to come to grips with the complexity of the notion and sense of the American mission.

*The Mission and the World.* It should now be clear that there is more than one way in which America might carry out its mission of perfecting its values and institutions and transmitting them to other nations. The United States might intervene to support liberal and progressive movements in other countries or to oppose aggressive threats to democratic regimes. More often though, proponents of the idea of the American mission have argued that the United States might rely almost completely on the power of its example to bring all nations to an appreciation of the value of its idea of equality, liberty, justice, and morality. This is the model, previously mentioned, of "a city on a hill"—"liberty enlightening the world."

In early 1950, a group in the National Security Council drew up a report detailing the international siutation and proposing that the United States take various measures to oppose the extension of Soviet power. That document—National Security Council Policy Paper Number 68, "United States Objectives and Programs for National Security" frequently made use of arguments reminiscent of traditional notions of the American mission in its explanation of the United States' purpose in the world.

> By the same token, in relations between nations, the prime reliance of the free society is on the strength and appeal of its idea, and it feels no compulsion sooner or later to bring all societies into conformity with it. . . . The idea of slavery can only be overcome by the timely and persistent demonstration of the idea of freedom.

There is much in this document, NSC-68, prepared as rationalization and defense for the policy of containment that smacks of the influences described earlier in this essay. Most striking is the description of the essence of conflict in world politics as the competition between the Kremlin's "idea of slavery" whose "implacable purpose" is to eliminate the challenge of freedom which "is peculiarly and intolerably subversive of the idea of slavery." Political conflict is defined as the battle between the righteous and the wicked. But the righteous are now identified by their freedom, their tolerance of diversity, and the other aspects of democratic government. It is those in the Kremlin, the totalitarian masters of the idea of slavery, who wickedly oppose the purposes of the United States.

NSC-68 is an important statement of the American mission because it was an official rationalization at the highest levels of government for the United States taking an active role not only in opposing the "idea of slavery" but also in promoting the American "idea of freedom."

> In a shrinking world, which now faces the threat of atomic warfare, it is not an adequate objective merely to check the Kremlin design, for the absence of order among nations is becoming less and less tolerable. This fact imposes on us in our interests, the responsibility of world leadership. It demands that we make the attempt, and accept the risks inherent in it, to bring about order and justice by means consistent with the principles of freedom and democracy.

It was not something new to suggest that the United States should actively seek to promote its values. There have always been those who believed that the American mission required American intervention in the affairs of other nations to foster democratic values and republican government. During the 1840s, for example, a "Young America" movement—somewhat akin to its nationalistic counterparts in Europe—was begun in the United States and proposed active intervention against absolutist governments in Europe.[13]

The period of the 1840s was a particularly intoxicating one for the American people. The United States was achieving its "Manifest Destiny" of filling a large portion of North America through conquest and treaty, and there were those who argued that all of Mexico, Central America, the Caribbean, and even South America should become part of the United States.[14] In such an atmosphere, the European rebellions of 1848 seemed ripe opportunities for the United States to take a lead in fostering republicanism and democracy. Nonetheless, the United States' role even at that most propitious time was limited to mere rhetorical support. Busy with continental expansion and experiencing sectional divisions that would lead to civil war, the United States did not have the capacity to intervene materially despite widespread enthusiasm for events in Europe. That is what Louis Kossuth discovered during his American tour of the early 1850s. There was no lack of support for his cause of Hungarian independence, but the support was mostly emotional—a lovely show of parades and banquets with little money raised and no official interference in Hungarian affairs offered by the United States.

It was not until the end of the nineteenth century that the United

States had the power necessary to adopt an interventionist notion of the American mission in the practice of its foreign policy. Wedded to American power, notions of the American mission might have a material as well as spiritual or intellectual influence in other countries. During the last ninety years, the United States has taken (and largely released) a Pacific and Caribbean empire, participated in two World Wars and a number of more localized conflicts, and attempted, with a brief exception, to exercise a position of leadership in world affairs. The idea of mission has continued to appear in discussions of how the United States should undertake its role as a powerful nation.

Turn-of-the-century American imperialists like Admiral Mahan, Theodore Roosevelt, and Senator Albert Beveridge wrote of a notion of mission which was at once racist, nationalist, and religiously based. Taking their cue from the likes of the Reverend Josiah Strong who in his popular book *Our Country* (1885) asked, "Does it not look as if God were not only preparing in our Anglo-Saxon civilization the die with which to stamp the peoples of the earth, but as if he were massing behind that die the mighty power with which to press it," the imperialists claimed to see a rivalry of races that could only be abated by the establishment of a moral law. There is involved in such arguments a concept of a naturally-ordained stewardship which must be assumed by those who are most morally fit, a responsibility to civilize, Christianize, and democratize less fortunate peoples.*[15]*

Notions of racial superiority and moral duty (in addition to Mahan's theories of the importance of American sea power) conditioned the United States in the last decade of the nineteenth century to take a Pacific and Caribbean empire. Perhaps the most notable example of this kind of missionary spirit is the famous episode during which President William McKinley claimed that God had mystically instructed him that the United States must take the Philippines, instruct and Christianize the Filipinos (never mind that in a former Spanish colony many people were Roman Catholics) and bring them the uplifting experience of American tutelage.

All of this seems to the present-day observer to represent a darker side of the American idea of mission, one that is fraught with racism, intolerance, and an arrogant thirst for power. It seems noble to offer ourselves as an example of morality and civic virtue and to hope our example will lead others to achieve our happy condition. On the other hand, it seems shameful to say that our special virtue is due to the natural dominance of the Anglo-Saxon race and the Protestant religion reaching its highest expression in the assumption of a stewardship by our country. The history of World War II has discredited ideologies of racial superiority, but there is an inevitable temptation of arrogance in an idea like the American mission which attributes unique virtue to a single state or nation.

There are commentators on the American mission who maintain that the expansionist, power-seeking, selfish ideologies which provided rationalizations for Manifest Destiny and imperialism, though messianic in tone, were not true expressions of the sense of mission arising from the American character.[16] Their argument is that the only true reflection of the missionary spirit of the American people is given witness by the less apparently selfish attempts on the part of the United States to inspire, aid, and encourage other nations in their struggle for liberty and democracy and to help themselves improve themselves materially. The position of these commentators is that the Good Neighbor Policy, the Marshall Plan, and the Peace Corps were undertaken as true expressions of the American mission. Episodes of imperialism, racial smugness, and cultural arrogance were not and, therefore, could not be maintained over a long period of time.

Jimmy Carter, for example, during his 1976 campaign for the presidency declared that our foreign policy "should be as open and honest and decent and compassionate as the American people themselves are." For, he contended, "in every foreign venture that has failed. . .our Government forged ahead without consulting the American people, and did things that were contrary to our basic character."[17] In his litany of things that the government had done in contradiction of our basic character Carter included the war in Vietnam and American military activities in Cambodia. It would be comforting to think that the American experience in Indo-China had been a gruesome mistake, the result of the manipulation of the policy process by wrong-thinking officials of the government, that all episodes in our history which do not, in retrospect, stir unanimous feelings of national pride were not reflective of the essentially good American people.

Bernard Brodie may be closer to the mark. He states in *War and Politics* that the United States became involved in Vietnam, in part, as an attempt to pursue the traditional American mission of doing good in the world and opposing repression and injustice.[18] As we tired of the war in Vietnam, many questioned the morality of the war, the bombings, the napalm and defoliants, the seeming abuse of the governmental processes through which we became involved in the war, and the support given at great cost to an apparently repressive and unpopular regime. But initially our entry into the conflict was widely accepted and hailed as part of our duty, part of our mission to protect freedom from the incursions of aggressive communism.

The tradition of the idea of the American mission is of necessity a conceit, a noble sounding but haughty myth. Ralph Gabriel, a historian who counted the idea of mission as one of the three basic doctrines of the American democratic faith—along with individualism and a belief in moral rectitude based on natural right—argued that ideas arise out of social situations and persist because they possess some utility. The idea of the American mission has proved useful in different ways and under different circumstances.

In the early days of the Republic, the idea and sense of mission fulfilled at least three functions. First, it provided a sense of unity in purpose in a nation that was founded largely on the worship of the individual. Second, the notion that the new nation would be the agent of redemption for the world lent the young and growing United States a sense of legitimacy vis-a-vis the established European states. Finally, the sense of mission helped to provide meaning to the lives of individuals by linking them and their often difficult lives with the unfolding of global destiny. In short, the idea and sense of the American mission provided Americans with a sense of superiority to other nations. Such a sense supports the sentiments of national and racial pride which may be necessary for the development of any policy.[19]

However, for a state which has come to a position of strength the sense of mission takes on additional purposes including the rationalization and justification of foreign policies. The trouble is that the notion of mission is flexible enough to admit of a number of interpretations. It has been noted above that there have been differences of opinion about how the mission is to be carried out—passively, through the power of example, or actively through economic, political, diplomatic, or military intervention. In addition, the ends of the mission—the preservation and promotion of liberal political principles and institutions—are somewhat imprecisely defined. E.M. Burns counts in his book *The American Idea of Mission* at least five more or less distinct values which missionary America is duty bound to propagate: liberty, equality, democracy, peace, and prosperity.[20] In domestic politics, we have not been able to reconcile adequately the frequently contradictory claims of these values. It is not surprising, therefore, that relatively reasonable people might disagree about how best to promote these virtues in other countries.

The result, of course, is that advocates of almost any position in the debate on a given foreign policy issue may claim the advantage of standing in the tradition of the mission of the American people. Both imperialists and anti-imperialists at the turn of the century, Albert Beveridge and William Jennings Bryan, for example, phrased their arguments in terms of the American mission, and most were probably quite sincere in believing that they knew best how to fulfill America's mission. In a similar manner, opponents and supporters of American involvement in the war in Vietnam claimed the sanctity of American values and accused those with whom they disagreed of being disloyal to America's duty. In a more recent debate, the question of the proper nature of American relations with so-called "authoritarian" regimes has called some to consider the demands of the American mission. Can the United States be true to its mission while supporting repressive regimes like those in South Korea and the Philippines or does the necessity of resisting and counteracting the designs of Soviet communism require cooperation with distasteful "authoritarian" regimes?

There is a fairly complex process in operation here. On the one hand, the views of the national interest that various individuals hold will affect their interpretations of the demands of the tradition of the American mission[21] and many people will defend the positions they take by relying on the elements of that tradition which they have found personally most persuasive. On the other hand, it is probably inevitable that statesmen and politicians in a democracy will defend their foreign policies in terms of moral appeals. Even a relatively "realistic" statesman like Henry Kissinger found the need at times during his tenure as Secretary of State to speak of the "moral foundations" of American foreign policy.[22] Whether the envocation of the notion of the American mission is sincere or cynical, the result of linking sometimes contradictory conceptions of the mission to foreign policy positions which ultimately are derived from evaluations of the demands of the national interest is a degree of confusion, detracting from a well-considered discussion of American policy.

What is more, devotion to the idea of the American mission has made it difficult to develop adequate concepts of and approaches to the demands of a successful foreign policy. The essence of the idea of the American mission (and it is probably impossible to speak in more precise terms) is that the United States is a country of singular virtue and that the American example should and can and likely will be followed by other nations. The upshot of this is that Americans have expected every revolution would follow in our path, and we have frequently been frustrated when promising events in other lands did not develop according to our model. The French Revolution gave way to the Reign of Terror, the revolt of Latin America against Spain to instability and authoritarian regimes, the Russian Revolution to Soviet Communism, and the liberation of the Third World to localized brands of socialism and Marxism. The Marshall Plan was a success in preserving free government in Europe, but foreign aid, the Alliance for Progress, and the Peace Corps have not caused the proliferation of liberal, democratic republics in the Third World. The frustrated American reaction has often been to pronounce a curse upon the incorrigible world and to hold little hope for our relations with much of the rest of the world.

The American model cannot be easily duplicated in other settings. The idea of mission is based, in part, on belief that the United States enjoyed a unique origin. That is true. Our revolution brought about a horizontal shift of sovereignty from Britain to the United States. But there was no vertical transfer of power from one group within the United States to another. The United States had no truly feudal period, no democratizing revolution, and in this respect our revolt was far different from the French or the Russian revolution. Also, prosperity for most individuals has been readily attainable throughout most of our history. Relatively widespread abundance is another fact of American history that has not been characteristic of very many states. Americans, while recognizing unique blessings, have not always recognized that those blessings have been partially responsible for the atypical development of the United States. The American experience cannot be transplanted wholesale in countries which have shared so little of that experience. To expect, for example, that grants of economic development assistance would lead to the evolution of democratic societies in the Third World is to neglect the lessons of the history of the United States. To hope that our more or less patient tutelage will easily cause greater respect for human rights in Latin America is to ignore the persistent strength of a class system that did not evaporate when independence was gained from Spain, a class system which American history leaves us ill-prepared to understand.

The continued influence of the idea of the American mission, thus, may present a number of difficulties for United States foreign policy. Various interpretations of the idea, whether cynically or sincerely held, can confuse and debase the public debate on the ends of foreign policy, limiting the possibility for the reasoned consideration of where the interests of the United States lie. An untempered belief in the applicability of the American model may lead to frustration and inconsistency in foreign affairs. The notion that the United States as the champion of the "idea of freedom" is engaged in inevitable conflict with the "idea of slavery" and that this conflict is the essence of international danger can blind us both to the possibility of accommodation and to the complex nature of the interests which motivate states and which also may lead to international friction. Finally, the sense of mission may become perverse. Pride in our nation and the belief in America's special virtue and destiny may in some times appear as arrogance, racism, intolerance, and belligerent jingoism. These are American characteristics which enlighten no one and do not provide a model for the world.

This is not to suggest that we could (or even should) jettison the sense of the American mission. It is quite likely that a democratic nation cannot maintain its vitality as a society without a sense of purpose. And it is just as likely that democratic statesmen will not be able to maintain the popular support without which they cannot sustain their policies, if those policies are blatantly cynical and divorced from basic American values. The seeming inevitability of linking a democracy's foreign policy with its moral purposes has been previously mentioned.

What is needed is not the rejection of the American mission, but rather a modest application of the mission. We should recognize, first of all, the limited ability of the United States to make the world over in its own image and reject the temptation to recoil in frustration when we are disappointed by developments in other countries. This may be especially important as we put the experience of Vietnam behind and act to assert American power again. In addition, Americans must be aware of the validity and importance of the moral claims of other cultures. For example, the concept of the individual and his rights does not have the same importance in many societies which is accorded to it in the West, but those same societies often have a more highly developed and also praiseworthy sense of community than Western societies do. Much of the American message of liberty, equality, and democracy is of exceptional worth, but these values should be balanced against other also worthy values.

The idea of the American mission has been one of several traditions which have influenced American foreign policy. If the rhetoric of Presidents Carter and Reagan is at all a useful guide, it is a sentiment which will continue to appeal to the American people and an idea which will affect the manner in which American statesmen view the world. Modestly considered and applied, the American mission might be part of a public philosophy which animates a vital society and a successful foreign policy. Unchecked, however, the notion of the American mission might easily degenerate into pernicious, yet impotent moralism which would leave the United States less able to react to the dynamics of the contending interests of various states and unwilling to respond to the moral challenge posed by the values and cultures of other societies and cultures.

# II. SOURCES OF AMERICAN VALUES

## CHAPTER TWO
## 1. CHRISTIAN REALISM AND
## AMERICAN VALUES
### Daniel G. Lang

Thoughtful observers have, for some time, noted that the West has become uncertain of its purpose, unsure of its place in the scheme of things. The emergence of German Nazism and Soviet Communism in the interwar period, based as they were on implicit criticisms of liberal democracy, challenged the liberals' dream of an international order of "free and equal nations, each nation consisting of free and equal men and women."[1] The tide of history moving toward universal reason and progress, in which the classic nineteenth century liberal placed such faith, had turned and given way to other, darker waves. Thus Walter Lippmann, writing in the early 1950s, warned that "the liberal democracies have been tried and found wanting—found wanting not only in their capacity to govern successfully in this period of wars and upheavals, but also in their ability to defend and maintain the political philosophy that underlies the liberal way of life."[2] The eclipse of the public philosophy—"the traditions of civility"—Lippmann warned would lead to the dissolution of the West itself.

The identity crisis brought on by such criticisms of the liberal idea and the emergence of regimes based, at least in part, on these criticisms posed serious questions for the Western states, particularly for the United States which assumed leadership of the West during World War II. What "public philosophy" would guide our actions in our international relations? If we were not engaged in making the liberal dream come true, what did we stand for? Such questions manifested themselves in the realist-idealist debate which dominated international relations theory in the 1940s and 1950s. The realists themselves attacked many of the assumptions which had animated the liberal democracies prior to World

War I. Yet most of those writing in the realist school wrote as friends of liberal democracy, their writings intended, in part, to teach liberals how to save themselves from being swept away by the shifting tide.

The realists, for example, uncovered a pacifist strain in liberalism which, ironically, made international relations less stable by inviting attack. On the other hand, they noted a streak of dogmatic ruthlessness in liberalism, particularly in the American variety, which tended to make its wars "moral crusades." Heavy reliance on the moods of mass opinion as a guide for policy only made these problems worse. Finally, the realists found liberals seeking to replace "political man" with "rational man" or with "economic man." Thus realists accused liberal idealists of refusing to recognize that ours is necessarily a world of conflict, opposing interests, and coercion. Peace, if possible at all, would be established only on the basis of a power equilibrium managed by ever-vigilant statesmen; it would not emerge by merely hoping that states would adhere to the dictates of international law, international organization, or world public opinion. In short, the realists argued that force is a necessary instrument in a state's foreign policy, but that such force must be directed to the achievement of limited, political objectives defined in terms of the national interest. These objectives stand above and are meant to temper the vagaries of public opinion. The general public, educated to this view, would understand that most questions of foreign policy ought to be left in the hands of diplomats; statesmen, one hoped, would in the pursuit of the national interest act in accord with the "classical and medieval virtue of prudence," as Hans Morgenthau put it in his *Politics Among Nations.*[3]

In calling forth the ancient and medieval virtue of prudence realists like Morgenthau indicated that they were not entirely comfortable with the relentless realism they seemed to advocate. E. H. Carr, one of the first to elaborate the realist-idealist theme, noted in *The Twenty Years' Crisis* that a too-consistent realism which sees political matters simply in terms of rivalry, historical determinism, and coercion leaves no room for moral judgments nor does it provide a basis for action. If all relations between people are reduced to questions of power, then there is not, in principle, any reason to prefer liberal democracy over any other way of life. Nor is it clear why statesmen ought to try to preserve human life, except in terms of inchoate drives which cause men to do so in spite of themselves. Recognizing this, realists like John Herz, Martin Wight, and Reinhold Niebuhr tended to invoke some version of the moral order as a basis for judging and acting.[4]

Realists, then did have notions about the way that international relations ought to be managed and the way that citizens ought to conduct themselves. Curiously enough their views tended to resemble the set of teachings concerning prudence, statesmanship, and war which formed a central core of the "Great Tradition" of Western civilization. Yet it goes without saying that the modern era differs in important ways from the ancient or medieval eras. Those differences may make it more difficult to exercise prudence or statesmanship as the Great Tradition would have understood it, or they may point political leaders in directions unanticipated in earlier times. In this essay, I want to examine some of the components of the traditional view of prudence, then to discuss several trends in the modern era which limit its exercise, and finally to suggest some of the ways in which prudence understood as "enlightened self-interest" may provide a guide in the conduct of contemporary international relations.

Aristotle defined prudence or practical wisdom as "a true and reasoned state or capacity to act with regard to the things that are good or bad for man."[5] Prudent men act both for their own good and for that of their fellow citizens generally. Since the authority to act for others lies in the realm of the political, prudence is preeminently the virtue possible in political leaders, legislators, or self-governing citizens. And because prudence concerns itself with both goodness and action, it is the virtue which provides a bridge between knowing and doing. It moves from abstract and general principles to their embodiment in particular situations, for "the work of man is achieved only in accordance with practical wisdom as well as with moral virtue; for virtue makes us aim at the right mark, and practical wisdom makes us take the right means."[6]

The man of practical wisdom is one who is capable of deliberating, but he does not deliberate about things "that are invariable, or about things that it is impossible for him to do."[7] Prudence, then, is an intellectual virtue, but because it is concerned with doing, it cannot exist without moral virtue, and its proper exercise depends on the cultivation of such moral virtues as courage, temperance, and justice. These moral virtues are learned habits and dispositions which guide practical wisdom and allow it to determine its choices. With self-mastery comes greater freedom to choose, greater opportunity to choose wisely, and greater ability to act in accord with chosen policy. Good regimes, according to ancient political science, are those which tend to produce and be ruled by prudent men. To produce such men would require stern laws, rigorous and comprehensive programs of education, severe restrictions on economic activity, and the strict regulation of much that we now deem as private.[8] Even so, ancient political science taught that the emergence of good regimes depended on certain fortuitous coincidences or accidents largely beyond the control of statesmen. While politics could bring a measure of happiness to human life, the deepest problems of human existence could not, finally, be met on the political level.

Aristotle is, then, careful to point out that while prudence is an intellectual virtue, it is not the highest one. Practical wisdom, he says, is concerned with "things human and things about which it is possible to deliberate," but "it would be strange to think that the art of politics or practical wisdom is the best knowledge, since man is not the best thing in the world."⁹ Thus, while Aristotle praises the political life, he points to an even higher way of life than the political, namely the philosophic or contemplative life, which concerns itself with what is eternal. There are limits to politics and knowing this ushers in moderate expectations about how far human nature may be transformed by political efforts to meet man's deepest problems.

Though the Christian Fathers differed with Greek philosophy in important respects, they did preserve this insight. They taught that, for all its imperfections, civil society is a great good and ought to be preserved as such, though one ought not to conclude from this that civil society can answer the deepest dilemmas of human existence. In the words of the American Catholic, John Courtney Murray, this means that: "Society and the state are understood to be natural institutions with their relatively autonomous ends or purposes, which are predesigned in broad outline in the social and political nature of man, as understood in its concrete completeness through reflection and historical experience. These purposes are public, not private. They are, therefore, strictly limited."¹⁰

The collection of people who make up those institutions are neither a choir of angels nor a pack of wolves; with Pascal, the man of practical wisdom recognizes that "man is neither angel nor brute, and the unfortunate thing is that he who would act the angel acts the brute."¹¹ What is possible for such communities is the establishment and maintenance of a civilized way of life distinguishable from the chaos of barbarism. That effort, however, necessitates the use of force since law and justice require force to vindicate them. As Pascal observed, "Justice without might is helpless; might without justice is tyrannical. . .We must then combine justice and might, and for this end make what is just strong, or what is strong just."¹²

For Reinhold Niebuhr and the others who founded the journal *Christianity and Crisis* in the early 1940s this was the issue posed by the rise of Hitler and the Third Reich. In the journal's first issue, written when Great Britain alone confronted Nazi power, Niebuhr described the Germans' descent into barbarism and made clear that "there are historic situations in which refusal to defend the inheritance of a civilization, however imperfect, against tyranny and aggression, may result in consequences worse than war."¹³ Though the Western states were imperfect instruments of justice, it would be a "perverse moralism" which refused to see any moral difference between Nazi Germany and England. Thus *Christianity and Crisis* attacked both the liberal pacifists whose principle of non-violence in effect kept them from discerning essential differences between civilization and barbarism, and the isolationist nationalists who wanted to propel America to the first rank of nations by letting the other major powers deplete each other's strength through war. Instead the journal argued that the proper course for the United States, the counsel of prudence, was to prepare for war. Against the self-righteousness of the pacifists and the nationalists, a *Christianity and Crisis* editorial proclaimed that "the moment when an imperfect man gives himself to a necessary fight for the maintaining of a decent life for the world, he takes another step toward the triumph of justice in his own life." [4] The war was not one of absolute good against absolute evil; it was, however, one of genuine good against genuine evil. Consequently one might find actions on both sides blame- or praiseworthy without altering one's general view of the conflict. Thus it was entirely consistent for the journal's editors, while urging the defense of Western civilization, also to protest the internment of Japanese-Americans in detention camps or the Allies' policy of obliteration bombing as unjust, although such judgments provoked readers' protests.

The view put forward by Niebuhr and the others reflected the traditional Western teaching about war. For the Christian Fathers, like Augustine, wars are an inevitable evil which grow out of human avarice and lust for domination; no amount of tinkering will alter that fact. For Augustine, war may be an instrument of punishment imposed on a state and its rulers when their behavior is such that it violates even the limited standards of earthly justice. Yet such punishment will only be a faint approximation of justice and the innocent will surely suffer as well as the guilty. Certainly the Belgians suffered much in World War II at the hands of Germans and Allies alike, though they sought to remain a neutral country. Moreover, Augustine recognized that in the absence of an impartial judge, each state becomes judge in its own case, making it easy to turn punitive action into unjust wars for revenge, greed, or conquest. War is always an evil, though it may be necessary to prevent or punish worse evils. Abraham Lincoln was willing to risk war rather than allow the extension of slavery into the territories; yet we find him in the Second Inaugural Address reminding his countrymen that it was the establishment of *American* slavery which brought on the scourge of war though sectional attachment to that institution provided the immediate cause of war. Both parties invoked God's aid against the other, "yet neither has been answered fully." The humility which comes in recognizing that God is not wholly on one side or the other leads to striving to act "with malice toward none; with charity for all" to set out to achieve a just and lasting peace.

Out of the concern to ally justice and might and the desire to mitigate in some small way the effects of international anarchy, the Church Fathers elaborated what became known as the just war doctrine. They attempted to distinguish (1) defensive war, which is always just, (2) just offensive war, which endeavors to rectify some wrong committed against one state by another or another's citizens, and (3) unjust offensive wars, which must be resisted. States should enter war only as a last resort after peaceful efforts to reconcile differences have been exhausted. Once a war has started, states ought to conduct their side of the war guided by rules of proportion and discrimination. In no case is calling for unconditional surrender a proportionate righting of a wrong; and in all cases the intent of the just war theory is to cast the terms of public debate and understanding in terms of "limited war."[15] This means that states ought to seek achievable objectives and must subordinate military force to those political objectives. Failure to do this results either in a program of mindless destruction for its own sake, or in an increasingly violent effort to impose politically unobtainable solutions. Conceived of as an extension of prudence, the just war theory would engage rulers in a process of moral reasoning in which the possible goods to be achieved would be weighed against the attending inevitable evils, with success an important consideration. For example, early critics of the United States' involvement in the Vietnamese War judged the United States' action imprudent—George Kennan called it "the wrong war in the wrong place at the wrong time"—not out of any love for the North Vietnamese or any hatred of the United States, but because they believed that our objectives there were unclear and/or unattainable. The United States' action reflected a loss of a sense of proportion which might not have occurred had political leaders thought more seriously about what they wanted to achieve in Vietnam, what the costs might be and whether the United States was capable of doing what was necessary for success.[16]

The ancients and such Church Fathers as Augustine and Thomas Aquinas presented prudence as an aristocratic virtue, implying an excellence of understanding and self-mastery of which few were capable, but which many were to respect. In allowing the prudent ruler to be judge in his own case, they recognized that ambition and arrogance might tempt the ruler to confuse or ignore just war criteria. Yet the potential rewards of placing such a heavy burden on statesmanship seemed to them worth the possible risks.

This view contrasts significantly with much contemporary American theory on the practice of statesmanship. American leaders may practice statesmanship as the tradition prescribes, yet they do not seem to do so self-consciously, and they do not often publicly defend their actions in its terms. This disjunction leads to inconsistency, lack of confidence by the leadership in their judgments, and eventual public disenchantment with its institutions.[17]

The disestablishment of prudence as an essential feature of the public philosophy is traceable to several trends characteristic of modernity in general. One such development was "the great democratic revolution" of the seventeenth and eighteenth centuries, the effects of which Alexis de Tocqueville set out to describe in *Democracy in America*. He found that one feature of democracy in America was the absence of the pursuit of "lofty" objects in American life. Whereas the nobility in aristocracies had the desire and the leisure to seek greatness, the American middle class was generally so concerned with business that its members did not pursue higher aims. The democratic passion for equality and the busyness of the middle class with mundane matters made it unlikely that aristocratic virtues would persist, though Tocqueville thought that lawyers could act in a way as a "natural aristocracy." Democratic societies are suspicious of wealth and claims of privilege, and so force these to give an account of themselves in democratic terms. Henry Kissinger suggests that one reason why the late Nelson Rockefeller failed to win the presidency was that he was a Rockefeller. Though he possessed the qualities of courage, vision, and persistence that are "the touchstones of leadership," his wealth and the privileges it accorded him in an egalitarian milieu made him profoundly ambivalent about his place in it: "He wanted assurance that he had transcended what was inherently ambiguous: that his career was due to merit and not wealth, that he had earned it by achievement and not acquired it by inheritance. In countries with aristocratic traditions—in Great Britain, for example, until well after World War II—an upper class moved in and out of high office convinced that public responsibility was theirs by right. Merit was assumed. But in the United States, the scions of great families are extremely sensitive to the charge of acquiring power through the visible exercise of influence or wealth; they believe that they must earn their office in their own right."[18] In addition to this ambivalence about holding power, an attribute one does not usually find in aristocracies, Rockefeller is said to have believed that every problem had a solution if only one worked on it long enough. In this lack of reserve or moderation, which is the very antithesis of aristocratic prudence, Rockefeller proved to have been typically American. His approach also suggests some of the limitations of forms of American conservatism in contrast with the traditional Western conservatism of Edmund Burke.

Democracies, then, are unlikely to engender aristocratic virtues like prudence, which has important consequences for foreign relations. For Tocqueville, successful foreign policy requires perseverence, secrecy, patience, and skillful regulation of the details of important undertakings. These are qualities which belong to an individual or to an aristocracy, but there is in democracies a propensity to "obey impulse rather than prudence, and to abandon a mature design for the gratification of a momentary passion." Fortunately, the prudent Washington had, in his Farewell Address, laid down a broad policy of isolation which made the United States' foreign policy consist more in abstaining than in acting, thus saving the new nation from its worst self."￼ Now that the United States is a leading power in world affairs, Tocqueville's observations strike us by their prescience. It is certainly not clear that mass democracies can easily set forth and pursue limited political objectives; instead they induce leaders to explain their policies in unlimited (and unachievable) terms. For a time following World War II, bipartisanship in foreign policy provided a buffer which tended to preserve foreign policy from the ups and downs of public opinion, but that buffer has since disappeared. The State Department, which once acted with some authority in these matters, now competes, often at a disadvantage, with presidential staff in the National Security Council.

A second development in modernity has been the growth of modern science and technology, which has circumscribed statesmanship by narrowing the margin of error and by encouraging the substitution of science for prudence. In an age of nuclear and biological weapons with unknown destructive potential, it seems irrelevant to some, and suicidal to others, to speak of limited war or just war. Yet political leaders must give some account of the ends such weapons might serve. When in 1980 the Carter administration shifted its nuclear targeting strategy from aiming at cities to aiming at military targets—moving from "assured destruction" to "war fighting" or "damage limitation"—it followed the logic of "flexible response" advocated by Secretary McNamara under President Kennedy and Secretary Schlesinger under President Ford. At its heart this is an effort to make limited war possible and deterrence credible, even at the level of nuclear arms. To some this licenses nuclear war, just as arms control agreements license arms races insofar as wars or arms races are not abolished altogether. Others argue that by making the nuclear threat more credible, the likelihood of actual use is reduced. But deterrence as a policy aim, particularly in its "assured destruction" form, also rests on morally dubious foundations. Leaders must proclaim their intention to destroy enemy populations in magnitudes much larger than the rules of proportionality or discrimination justify in order not to have to use nuclear weapons in the first place. On the other hand, renouncing the intention to use nuclear weapons might be tantamount to surrender. It is little wonder that presidents prefer to leave the whole problem in the hands of systems analysts and military strategists. Against all this the traditional teaching insists that leaders have or develop options other than "either red or dead," ever mindful that military science must be subordinated to broader political and diplomatic objectives.

Another example of the way that science and technology have made statesmanship difficult can be seen in the less developed countries whose ways of life have been profoundly unsettled, as recent events in Iran suggests. These new states often seem unable to cope with the rapid changes they are undergoing, and sometimes this very instability and weakness brings on war. The Congo crisis of the early 1960s was created by the hasty departure of Belgian professionals which left the colony virtually without a state apparatus. Internecine fighting among various factions soon broke out, the superpowers took sides, but both eventually supported the entry of United Nations forces to impose order. Neither the United States nor the Soviet Union wanted to confront each other over the Congo—hence their willingness to let the United Nations handle the situation. Yet both found themselves pulled into a vacuum created by Congo's weakness. Diplomacy, which is what the traditional teaching on statesmanship and war was designed to encourage, is made difficult when one is trying to negotiate with a government so weak and with so little sense of identity that its promises cannot be taken seriously. Present-day Lebanon has so slight a sense of national identity and its government so little authority that it could hardly be described as a reliable diplomatic bargaining partner. That life in weak states like Lebanon may be approaching the chaos of barbarism does provide grounds justifiable for action, though not necessarily war. Indeed, when one looks at much of the activity of the United Nations and other agencies of functionalism, one can see that their activity is intended, at least in part, to build up or strengthen some of these weak states. According to I. L. Claude, Jr., the assumption underlying such activities is that "the greatest danger to world peace in this generation may derive not from deliberate acts of aggression but from inadvertent entanglement in rivalry. The strengthening of the capacity of weak states and strong alike to avoid what they do not want to do, to move from predicament to policy, will enchance the prospects for global order."[20]

A third development in modernity is the rise of ideology. The notion that prudence is the virtue which works within a range of possibilities and limitations is termed reactionary by those who claim either that everything is possible or that all is limited by the necessities of class conflict. When Edmund Burke condemned the "new politics" of the French Revolution as a violation of all counsels of prudence and as a total departure "from every one of the ideas and usages, religious, legal, moral, or social, or this civilized world," Thomas Paine cast him as an arch-enemy of progress, determined to hide people in the dark shadows of tradition and prejudice rather than to lead them into the daylight of reason.

Against the long tradition of philosophy beginning with Socrates which counselled prudence because of the inevitable gap between theory and practice, Karl Marx declared that philosophers "have only interpreted the world, in various ways; the point, however, is to change it." In the 1960s proponents of the "New Politics" sought to overthrow the "Establishment," rejecting out of hand any claim of experience or wisdom that members or detached interpreters of that Establishment might put forth. Ideology instructs the public mind to think in terms of inevitable progress, forces of absolute good contending against absolute evil, and the assertion of will to remake political reality in the service of some high ideal. American statesmen seem far more prone to explain their otherwise prudent actions in these exaggerated terms than in terms of the traditional view. The effect has been to push prudence out of sight.

Nevertheless there have been efforts to rescue prudence as a guide for statesmen and their American public, though with a less lofty character than it initially had and more in tune with American limitations. In the nineteenth century Alexis de Tocqueville defended the "principle of self-interest rightly understood," and in the twentieth century Reinhold Niebuhr defended "enlightened self-interest."

For Tocqueville the "great democratic revolution" was, above all, the triumph of the spirit of equality. As social conditions become more and more equal, men increasingly view themselves as disconnected atoms: they have no obligations, as equals, to their ancestors, their descendents, or their contemporaries. Americans have fought this solipsistic individualism by drawing men into political and civic associations where their individual interests are confronted with the interests of others, and by developing the general principle that a man may serve private and public interest at the same time. In aristocratic ages, the nobility "dwelt incessantly on the beauties of virtue," but in the United States "hardly anybody talks of the beauty of virtue, but they maintain that virtue is useful and prove it every day."[21] Americans may practice a kind of self-mastery, but will defend it as being useful for some other purpose than as a good in and of itself. Thus, keeping one's word gives one the reputation of being dependable, whether or not it engenders self-respect; or, acting for the common good causes certain rewards to fall on those who so act. Publius, in *The Federalist Papers,* argues that presidents should be allowed unlimited re-eligibility because a president whose ambition or greed might cause him to act against the interests of the nation might put off fulfilling those personal interests if he thought he could be president again: "if he could expect to prolong his honors by his good conduct, he might hesitate to sacrifice his appetite for them to his appetite for gain."[22] In this way the president is made to act both for the good of the country and for his own interests as well. Publius hopes that the Constitution will establish institutions which will induce men to rule well, but he does not seem to think that many will do so simply because ruling well is a good thing. Rather, by teaching men where their true interest lies, Publius hopes to turn private interest to public use.

This principle of self-interest rightly understood appeared to Tocqueville to be: "the best suited of all philosophical theories to the wants of the men of our time, and I regard it as their chief remaining security against themselves. Towards it, therefore, the minds of the moralists of our age should turn; even should they judge it to be incomplete, it must nevertheless be adopted as necessary."[23] This principle will not produce any great acts of self-denial, but suggests frequent small acts of self-sacrifice; it will not pull men to be excellent human beings, as the traditional teaching would, but it will at least make them relatively decent. It does not instill knowledge of highest statesmanship to those few who are capable of comprehending it, but instead offers guidance which is clear, sure, and understandable for the educated citizen. The proposal to tax gasoline and use the revenue generated to save the Social Security system appealed to some Americans because they found high-minded appeals for voluntary conservation ineffective. A gasoline tax makes it in our interest to use less gasoline because gas will cost us more to buy, and it will serve the interests of the country by reducing dependence on foreign oil and by reviving the Social Security system, thus illustrating Tocqueville's principle.

Tocqueville admits that this principle will not in itself make men virtuous, "but it disciplines a number of persons in habits of regularity, temperance, moderation, foresight, and self-command." These qualities at least resemble virtue. In the last analysis much depends on teaching men how best to understand their self-interest. Self-interest rightly understood is "not in all its parts self-evident," but men, if properly educated, "cannot fail to see it."[24] Such education lies near the heart of Tocqueville's work.

Though Reinhold Niebuhr begins with more explicitly theological premises he argues substantially for the same principle. Beginning with the Augustinian understanding that human life and human activities are inevitably tainted by sin, evil, and egoism, Niebuhr argues that selfishness and conflict are inevitable and ineradicable in human affairs. This gives an air of tragedy to politics and to prudence, which must choose between greater and lesser evils. It is the task of prudence to try to reduce coercion by "counseling the use of such types of coercion as are most compatible with the moral and rational factors in human society and by discriminating between the purposes and ends for which coercion is used."[25] The highest ends which prudence can serve are those which fall under the rubric of "enlightened self-interest": proximate justice at home and a careful attention to the requirements of self-preservation abroad, but with an understanding of the requirements of others as well. Although the power impulse of states is so strong and the sense of the human community is so weak, it is nevertheless important to establish the possibility that a nation may best serve the common good by following its own best interest, always mindful of man's limited capacity for self-sacrifice. Self-seeking, practiced too consistently without regard for the society in which men act must be self-defeating. A narrow definition of the national interest similarly leads to ultimate defeat, just as Napoleon's pursuit of world empire ultimately led to the collapse of Napoleon's France or as American isolationism during World War II might have done. Prudence as enlightened self-interest teaches this; it also teaches that the self needs other selves in order for it to be itself. In interpersonal relations we recognize this as love shared between husband and wife, family members, or friends. In intergroup relations prudence looks to an order of justice: giving each his due.

Such an understanding can inform the West's account of itself in the world. At home, the issue is one of proximate justice: absolute justice becomes more unlikely the more vigorously it is pursued. We can speak of ours as a decent way of life, though not as the best. "Democracy is social wisdom because though the common man isn't wise, he knows that his shoe pinches."[16] The establishment and maintenance of that social wisdom has proved to be more difficult than liberals and idealists had imagined, though the Framers themselves regarded their enterprise as a noble, but risky experiment. That that experiment is not easily replicated elsewhere does not necessarily make the experiment a failure.

Abroad, the United States must act for itself as a civilized community first, and yet it can act for international society as well by pursuing concurrent interests with others in that larger society. Niebuhr suggested that what peace the world has known in the postwar world has come about because of the balance of terror existing between the ideologically opposed adversaries in the Cold War. "A precarious nuclear peace, based on a "balance of terror" has been established in the world because the novel dimension of destructive capacity in nuclear weapons creates an identity between mutual interest and self-interest in the two contestants.[17] Neither side is willing to sacrifice its interests in the name of the world community and both lack sufficient mutual trust to work out much of a positive peace between them. But the ideological chasm between them has been bridged to a certain extent by some sense of responsibility for avoiding nuclear war. And ironically, this careful attention to self-preservation—to self-interest rightly understood—has obliquely served the interests of the world as a whole. Many have seen the Marshall Plan and to some extent the containment doctrine as an expression of the same principle. Clearly the United

States benefitted from the arrangement, but just as clearly so did the Europeans. To be sure, there is nothing automatic about the process so that when conditions change a new application of the principle may have to be worked out.

Nevertheless, because we are heirs and custodians of the higher tradition of prudence and statesmanship, we will at times feel pulled as Woodrow Wilson was when he protested the pettiness and mediocrity of boss and party politics in late 19th century American politics. To Wilson the politics of material interest which seemed to preoccupy the political parties prevented the rise of true statesmen to lead the people. Wilson longed for a time when men of the high stature of the Founding Fathers would again lead the country. Consequently he developed a theory of the presidency designed to liberate the president from the chains of petty politics so that he could speak to the great issues of the day. He spoke of a unique "life" relationship between president and the people in which the statesman as orator could "touch the imaginations of common men, give clear voice to their half-conscious longings, and inspire in a diverse multitude the zest for united action."[28] Thus could the popular statesman define the national purpose and give coherent direction to the opinion of the country. Wilson hoped that such popular statesmanship would provide for the exercise of something like prudence though cloaked in the robes of "public opinion." One sees the best expression of this in Wilson's campaign to mobilize the country's voters to put pressure on the Senate to ratify the treaty which would put the United States in the League of Nations. His fervent appeals to the general public to act out the highest possible motives in support of the League is quintessential Wilsonian statesmanship, yet one could not imagine an aristocratic Washington making such appeals. Ironically, Wilson's attempt to make statesmanship a central part of American government has made American statecraft less prudent by linking it so directly to public opinion, which limits discretion and flexibility. Rather than acting to restrain American tendencies to immoderation or legalism, Wilson's popular statesman fans the flames. Moreover, continual appeals to high principle unrealized in practice may produce disillusionment and cynicism more corrosive than that engendered by party politics. One wonders whether references to detente as a "new structure for peace," human rights as the core of American foreign policy, and energy conservation as "the moral equivalent of war" did not produce these same effects.

There is, then, real tension between prudence as aristocratic virtue and as democratic "enlightened self-interest." Nostalgia for the former ought not to make us overlook the relative absence of soil out of which such a noble plant might emerge. Benjamin Barber, commenting on the dearth of leadership, suggests that our dilemma is not an absence of leaders, but a paucity of values that might sustain leaders: "It is no good for us to go looking for leaders; we must first rediscover citizens."[29] But one does not easily tell the people that it is they who must be watched, as Washington himself discovered when he endeavored to keep the new nation out of the wars of the French Revolution.

The language of "enlightened self-interest" is plain, understated, cautious, and parochial. This is both its greatest strength and its greatest weakness. Thus the relatively sure guide of containment turned into exaggerated emphasis on the friendliness of the Soviet Union, which in turn gave way to cynicism or deep pessimism when that friendship soured; and human rights as a guide proved elusive at best, becoming all thing to all men. This tendency to excess does not necessarily invalidate each of these as a valid "public philosophy," but it does suggest that a doctrine of restraint and of necessity ought to be part of the "public philosophy" if it is to be reliable. "Enlightened self-interest" reminds us that enlightenment is possible, but that there is something stubborn about self-interest which must also be taken into account.

# CHAPTER THREE
## 2. CLASSICAL SOURCES OF AMERICAN VALUES
### Alan Pino

In discussing the question of the political morality of liberal regimes Joseph Cropsey expresses astonishment that they characteristically "renounce the authority to impose legality or the conservation of the regime, on private men as the standard of some of those men's most powerful acts."[1] It was this Walter Lippmann was referring to in the 1950s, when he warned of the danger that liberal democratic regimes were facing as a result of their failure to develop what Cropsey calls "standards of political morality"[2] by which to judge and influence behaviour affecting the character of the regime. Lippmann believed that this failure had contributed to the widespread loss of the conviction that "there are certain obligations binding on all men who are committed to a free society,"[3] obligations which "only the willfully subversive can reject."[4] He argued that this sense of obligation had been sustained by natural law doctrines passed down to the West from the Stoics. They provided, he believed, along with Christianity, the basis for the idea of a rational order of things from which basic truths about man and society were drawn.

As a way of revitalizing the decayed political moralities of the western democracies he urged the recovery of these natural law precepts. He believed this a necessary first step to the establishment of a "public criterion of the true and the false. . ."that would show disinterested discrimination between good and bad in public life.

The problem with Lippmann's idea is that the very thinkers considered to be the founders of liberal and democratic thought—Hobbes, Locke, and Rousseau—helped to undermine an attachment to those very natural law precepts Lippmann sees a need to recover.

In fact, the modern reinterpretation of natural law beginning with Hobbes, transposes the community oriented thought of the older tradition to the level of the individual, and a concern for duties owed to the community or rights shared as part of it, to a question of natural rights belonging to individuals outside of society. The exaltation of the individual by these thinkers meant a corresponding depreciation of the idea of a universal law of right reason inhering in the nature of things. Thus there is a profound tension between the older tradition, grounded in the adherence to Aquinas' idea of natural law as what reason has been able to discern of God's eternal law, and the revision of the old view, provided by modern thinkers, which sees natural law as no more than the principles reason is able to find out when it considers the needs established by man's physical nature.

Indeed, modern political thought, beginning with Machiavelli, posits a view of the nature of man, the character and purpose of the public realm and its relation to the private realm that attempts to supplant the conception of these things developed by the Greeks, and perpetuated in the Christian tradition.

The ideas at the heart of this effort have resulted in the paradox that the two major strands of modern political thought, liberalism and utopianism have, by and large, been either non or antipolitical. In the liberal strain the political realm has not been rejected but has been seen as inferior to the private realm, where, liberalism argues, men can better express and fulfill themselves. In the utopian strands politics is rejected altogether. The political realm is seen to represent conflict and exploitation, both of which, utopian thought assures us, will be eliminated in the perfect societies history is bringing. Despite the wisdespread recognition of the shortcomings of the societies that have tried to realize one or another version of the utopian idea, the vision it holds out still retains a strong hold over men's minds and thus remains a dangerous threat to liberal societies.

While modern liberal theory has done admirably in providing a philosophical justification for individual freedom against the claims of the state, it has never developed a rational for using politics to cultivate the kinds of social character necessary to sustain a public philosophy committed to freedom. In order to do this, it must explore the possibility of recovering the insights of the Greek tradition about the relationship between politics and ethics. The heart of this insight is perhaps most clearly expressed in Plato's observation that constitutions do not arise from rocks or trees but from the character of the individuals who make up a regime.

I first want to describe briefly the central ideas of the Greek view of politics. Then I will turn to the nature of the revolution effected by Machiavelli and Hobbes and show how the ideas forged in this revolution have reverbrated through modern thought, significantly shaping the development of both liberal theory and utopian ideology. Finally I will consider the possibility of liberal theory recovering elements of the Greek perspective in order to build a philosophical basis for a regime committed to nurturing the kinds of virtues necessary for sustaining a free society.

The dispute between the ancients and moderns centers on the question whether politics can or should be guided by the purpose of developing virtue in society. The Greeks answered this question with an unqualified affirmation. They believed that only through political society can man fully and properly develop his distinctive capacities—reason and speech. The highest use of reason and speech resulted from community-spirited deliberation by men of the best character. They defined the best regime as that which embodies the truest idea of what is useful and just for a human community. The citizens shaped in accordance with this idea would tend to embody a corresponding excellence of character.[5] They did not think a community could leave the formation of character to the spontaneous, unplanned operation of private institutions. They argued that the kind of character shaped in private life would crucially influence the capacity for citizenship, that is, the ability to seek justice for the whole over the interest of the part. Thus they considered it imperative that the community use its political realm to encourage patterns of life in the private sphere conducive to the creation of the qualities most appropriate to the regime as a whole. In one sense, then, that of educating to virtue, they had a very broad view of what government should try to do. But the kinds of actions they considered it legitimate to take in achieving this end were limited by their view of human nature as fixed and imperfect. Educating to virtue did not mean transforming man's nature in order to create a perfect society.

The Greek conception of the role of political life placed great responsibility upon the statesman. He was charged with the task of balancing the competing interests struggling for power in the community with a view to realizing a common good beyond the mere utilitarian goal of maximizing the private happiness of the greatest number. He was to aim at a good in which competing claims were reconciled so as to create the proper balance of reason and passion within each citizen and therefore within the community as a whole.

Thus, for the Greeks, politics was ultimately in the service of ethics or the life of virtue. But the standards by which one decided which actions were virtuous and which were not could not be established in the political realm itself with its clash of forces competing for power. Rather, what constituted justice in society was seen to depend upon the philosopher. Only he, they argued, starting with a critique of the "accepted wisdom" of political society, could arrive at knowledge of the extent to which society's "truths" partake merely of opinion about things and to what extent they accurately express true knowledge about things, for only he, through a critical examination of conventional wisdom, has the possibility of attaining a vantage point sufficiently free of the compromises men must make in order to sustain life in community. They believed that this detached and elevated perspective would allow the philosopher to explore the universally valid questions about political things to which, they thought, certain universally valid answers were, in principle, possible.[6]

Thus, while the ultimate purpose of the political realm was to instill virtue, this realm remained under judgment of a higher, philosophical one which attested at the same time to the lower's nobility, and to its limits. In other words the ultimate subordination of politics to philosophy did not lead the Greeks to denigrate the political realm nor to try to impose the "universally valid answers" upon the world of practical affairs. Instead they made a distinction between theoretical and practical wisdom, the former involving the search for answers to the unchanging problems or questions posed by the nature of man and society, the latter involving the application of prudence by the politician to the everchanging factors present in individual situations.

In summary, the Greeks believed that man's nature was unchanging and imperfect and therefore that politics was limited in its possibilities. Nevertheless, while recognizing the limitations of all men, they believed a few were capable of achieving excellence of character, and that these had the responsibility to serve as models and guides for the development of those qualities of mind and body most appropriate for each citizen and for the community as a whole. Finally, they made a distinction between the theoretical knowledge of the philosopher, which was concerned with absolutes, and the practical knowledge of the politician, which modified those absolutes according to the demands of experience.

The attack on the Greek approach to ethics and politics begins with Machiavelli. He rejects the Greek idea that the contemplative life, philosophy, is devoted to an order of things that lies beyond the self-interest of communities and is thus necessary for understanding what is best for community and for the attainment of virtue. He substitutes for this the idea that wisdom consists in understanding that actions and ideas only partake of truth to the extent that they are useful for maintaining the polity. Machiavelli emphasizes the ability to manipulate appearances as the key to success in politics. He sees man not as the rational animal or the animal with the red cheeks—that is, capable of shame—but as the deceptive animal. Man uses his reason, according to Machiavelli, to satisfy his urgent and never ceasing desires. Machiavelli's answer to Plato's parable about the ring of Gyges—which deals with the question whether even the just man would not do evil if he could do it with impunity—is that of course he would. For goodness results only when society makes bad, that is, destructively self-centered actions, unprofitable.[7] Knowledge of the techniques for making men desire to do what is good for the political order is the highest knowledge the ruler or the philosopher can have. The distinction between opinion about the good and true knowledge of it is irrelevant to Machiavelli because that distinction has no bearing on the problem of acquiring and holding political power. He replaces the Greek aspiration to virtue based on knowledge of the good with the possibility of glory.

In opposition to the Greek idea of the connection between ethics and politics, Machiavelli tells us that we must make a choice between the two, for they are, he says, irreconcilable. If one chooses politics, then virtue must be defined in terms of the common good, which means the stability and glory of the regime. Virtue in private and public life have nothing to do with one another, in fact they are opposed. The good man and the good citizen do not coincide in the best or any other regime because establishing political order requires manipulation of men's passions, not the attainment of the Greek virtues. Men may wish to delude themselves into believing that their personal relations are guided by such motives as love and charity but this delusion depends ultimately on the social stability that proper management of the public realm brings. And this management is effected by appealing to the exceptional man's passion for glory and by channeling the selfish desire of the average man toward constructive ends.

Machiavelli does not believe politics can transform human nature. But he does believe politics or the highest of politicians—the political philosopher—can show men how to realize the good society without themselves becoming good. He argues that rigorous self-reform to develop virtue is fruitless because man is essentially a creature of his passions. Reason can see the need to guide them to produce social harmony. But knowledge is ultimately, to use Hobbes' phrase, only another form of the desire for power. It cannot help man to realize a nobler side of his nature; it can only show him how to control his baseness. Thus, for Machiavelli, while man's nature is "fixed", in that he cannot transcend self-interest, it is malleable, in that he can be brought to identify his self-interest with something beyond himself.[8]

For the Greeks the approach to absolute truth could only occur through the relative purification in the contemplative life of the cruder passions and opinions that were an inevitable part of the life of politics. They believed that success in the search for knowledge of, as opposed to opinion about, political things, required the acquisition of the virtues. Wisdom was not believed possible for a discordant soul.

As Strauss points out, Machiavelli rejects this idea of a connection between wisdom and moderation.[9] Correspondingly he rejects the idea that the truth of the contemplative life is distinct from the truth governing the life of action. For him the truth of the philosopher is the truth of the ruler. Thus, while the Greeks believed the truth about the good society would serve as a measure for judging the relative goodness of existing societies, Machiavelli implies that the true principles of political order can serve as handbook whose maxims can be directly applied to the changing reality of politics. Machiavelli does not develop a science of politics—that came later, as I shall show. But he does replace the Greek idea of theory as a principle of measurement with that of theory as a principle of action. He thus opens the door to the idea that reality can be made to conform to thought. Machiavelli's rejection of a just order of the soul by which to judge the proximate justice attainable in political life represents an early form of the idea, later fully developed in utopian thought, that the Greek distinction between theoretical and practical knowledge could be replaced by one between theoretical and applied knowledge. The full emergence of the latter view marked the beginning of the belief in the scientific treatment of society. It regarded society as a "laboratory" in which theories could be directly "tested."

For Hobbes men also desire to gain power over others—and thus glory—in order better to satisfy their passions. But beneath the desire for the ever-changing things of the world lies the greatest desire of all—for the condition which makes continued desiring possible—the desire for self-preservation. The purpose of the state or the public realm is to restrain the desire for glory in order to guarantee survival to pursue private appetites. The government is now envisioned as a referee whose purpose is not to cultivate excellence but to provide security.

Machiavelli retained some of the Greek concern for a hierarchy in society based on the possession of virtue, though he regarded virtues as primarily a means, rather than as ends in themselves. He thus retained, though in radically altered form, a standard for distinguishing the good from the mediocre citizen. With Hobbes, however, all criteria of public excellence are abandoned. The good citizen is simply one who does not, to use the negative formulation of which Hobbes is so fond, break the law. One may, in principle, be completely dissolute, consumed by the basest passions, a devil, in other words; but, as we know, rational devils can be brought to see how their self-interest depends on obeying rules common to all.[10]

The public realm for Hobbes is no longer the arena where men come together to deliberate and argue about what constitutes the common good, but the realm of the policeman and the umpire or judge. Their powers are indeed absolute, for Hobbes found divided authority not only illogical but an invitation to anarchy; but the ends they are to help achieve are limited.

Thus the concept of the all-powerful Leviathan was not a paradigm of the totalitarian state, interfering in every aspect of its citizens lives—quite the opposite. Hobbes intended in fact to empty the public realm of almost all content and to have it exercise its authority through the formal mechanism of rules. These would define the rights involved in the collisions that would inevitably result between individuals pursuing self-interested ends.

In other words the idea of a public philosophy was abhorrent to Hobbes because he believed such an idea would promote arguments about what constitutes a good society, and such arguments are what lead to the collapse of society into warring factions. Beneath the appearance of righteousness men display in championing their conceptions of the good is merely the desire for power. But the struggle for power can never be elevated by the great statesman, since there is nothing in man capable of elevation. Man, for Hobbes, is a mechanism of passions with reason merely a reckoner of consequences, and as Hannah Arendt has noted, when reason is conceived in this fashion, it ceases to be thought of as mind and becomes brain—simply another biological function.[11] Reason so conceived derives its knowledge only from the senses. The laws of nature are those rules that can be deduced by calculating the excess of pleasure over pain if all agree to abide by the same rules regulating behaviour. These, however, only become valid once men have formally bound themselves by contract in a civil society. Natural law is not revealed to man by God, nor does it inhere in the nature of human relationships, imposing obligations on men regardless of their situation. It originates in the individual's desire for self-preservation, in mere biological existence, and becomes obligatory only through an act of human artifice—the creation of a contract made by each party with a view strictly to his own self-interest.

Natural law provided, in pre-modern thought, the link to an absolute truth beyond society by which to judge society's claims and aspirations. Machiavelli—as mentioned—implicitly attacks the idea of such a truth; and Hobbes explicitly severs the connection between universal truths and human understanding by arguing in effect that if such truths exist man has no way of knowing them. For Hobbes the restraint man could place on his will through the artifice of society was limited by the strength of the self-interested passions. Indeed, he adopted St. Augustine's notion of the sinfulness of man with a vengeance. Through a systematic analysis of causes man can be understood and controlled, but not redeemed.

Enlightenment thought derives from Hobbes, not his profound skepticism, but his idea of reason as mere mechanical reckoning, and his conception of man as primarily the subject of egoistic desires, for which nature and society are seen as a means of fulfillment. Reason is seen as a means of arranging institutions to channel desire in order to bring them to fulfillment in socially constructive ways. Man is viewed as a subject capable of being analyzed and understood in the same way as nature. The good society thus becomes a question of rational social-engineering rather than of ethical maturity. The goal of politics then becomes the triumph of science, or, rather, the "analytical science of man," which will allow us to treat him as merely one of nature's processes, subject to the same casual laws.

Hobbes reflects an early form of the modern fascination with science and the belief in its power. But for him its power was primarily explanatory. It showed him that man was essentially a mechanism, matter in motion, but did not suggest to him possibilities for improvement. For Enlightenment thinkers, on the other hand, science, through its application to society, acquired a power to transform man's estate. If men would but yoke themselves to the power of enlightened reason, they could have hope of bringing about an "organic change in the way men conduct themselves," and thus realize the possibility of "transcending eternal [human] conflict." [12]

Leo Strauss has observed that a chief—possibly the defining—characteristic of modern thought is the conscious lowering of standards. [13] Machiavelli and Hobbes take the lowest common denominator of behaviour as their standard to achieve right order in society. It is a great paradox that with Enlightenment thought this lowered view of man results in a philosophy of the highest expectations.

This paradox can be explained, I think, as a consequence of two central ideas of modern thought: the first, evident in Machiavelli, is the idea of the malleability of human nature; [14] the second is the replacement of the distinction between theoretical and practical wisdom with that between theoretical and applied knowledge. [15] In fact it was the application of the principles of natural science to the idea of a malleable human nature that allowed the substitution of applied for practical knowledge.

Hobbes's idea of man as a mechanism of passions lends itself beautifully to the conviction that the application to a "human mechanism" of principles modeled on physics could produce a series of rigorous deductions connecting theory and practice. Reducing man to the status of a desiring machine meant that improvements in his condition could be expected to occur with the same regularity as improvements in science itself. It was this way of thinking, then, that allowed the transformation of a lowered view of man into the highest expectations for him. It further transformed the idea of theory as speculation about fundamental problems into what we now call ideology: the latter being, in the words of Hannah Arendt, "a system of thought which attempts to explain everything by deduction from a single premise, and which thus treats events as if they followed the same law as the logical exposition of an idea.''[16]

Hence it is not far from the early expression of high expectations, as in Condorcet's or even Kant's belief in history as a rational progression, to the Marxian view that history is moving from ''the domination of man by man,'' as reflected in bourgeois politics, to a world without politics, in which the traditional political problem of resolving conflicts between men asserting opposing claims is ''replaced by the administration of things.''[17] Marx culminates a movement to find meaning not in politics but in history, the result being that politics comes to be seen as a realm of necessity, a mere epiphenomenon of the historical process through which the ''good'' society is realized.

Marx pursues the implications, both of the idea of man's malleability and of the new distinction between theoretical and applied knowledge, to their logical conclusions. For Marx man ceases to have any kind of fixed nature. In an ironic perversion of the Greek idea, he sees man as a "social" animal in the sense that his nature is determined by the socio-economic arrangements prevailing at different stages in history. Man is perfectible, that is, capable of unselfishly devoting himself to the good of others, because the dynamics of history are perfecting the social and economic conditions from which his new nature will emerge.

The new distinction between theoretical and applied knowledge, evident in embryonic form in Machiavelli's rejection of truth beyond the political realm, and more fully developed in Hobbes' rigorous deduction of axioms of politics intended to form a handbook for the ruler, is transformed by Marx in his idea that theory only attains validity when it is applied to reality. Practice that embodies a true understanding of the forces of history is the only real philosophy. Thus one sees in Marx the attempt to use ideas to put an end to the need for the philosopher. He sought an end to the philosophical tradition conceived as an effort to explore fundamental questions regarding man and society because, like Hobbes, he realized the danger to any established order posed by the mind committed to explore freely the nature of things. Thus both men pay backhanded homage to the Greek recognition of the ultimate tension between philosophy and politics. The commitment to truth of the former is always a threat to the compromises with justice required in the latter. For the Greeks, the wisdom of the statesman tries to mediate between the two. For Marx, the statesman is no longer necessary because he (Marx) has replaced the old tension between philosophy and politics with that between the forces and the relations of production, a tension that will be resolved by history itself. There is no need for philosophers or politicians in Marx's paradise.

The other major line of modern thought which ''attempts to explain everything by deduction from a single premise," is expressed in the view that society is a problem for technical administration. The first to develop this conception was Saint Simon, whose influence is seen in Weber and in the modern positivist political science represented by Harold Lasswell. The ultimate end of these champions of the scientific management of society is, in the words of Laski, to "reorder the world" and produce the "immanent satisfaction of the masses." [18] For the believer in this version of the science of man the important tasks of government fall not to the statesman but to the technocratic expert who understands the complexities of rational administration. The political vocation is seen as subordinate to the realm concerned directly with the administration of society's needs. The modern state conceived in this way deals not with communities but with masses, that is, aggregations of isolated individuals for whom it exists to be responsive to demands for security and the well-being necessary to pursue the non-political aims of the "life process." [19]

Thus, modern thought, having begun by attempting to lower the Greek image of man, ends (at least in these utopian strands) by claiming to free man from the restraints of his own nature. Further, having begun by viewing politics as all encompassing, it ends by seeing man's freedom as consisting in his creation of a world in which politics is abolished altogether.

Liberalism's main similarity with utopian thought has been its sharing of the latter's assumption about the incompatibility of freedom and politics. But liberal thinkers, working with Hobbe's and the older tradition's idea of human nature as fixed and imperfect, did not try to abolish politics but to limit it. This shared assumption, however, has been a major source of weakness for liberalism in the struggle with utopian ideas and regimes. Utopian thought's vision of a world in which freedom, equality and justice can be realized by all men without conflict or sacrifice has seduced many when compared with liberalism's emphasis on limiting politics to preserve freedom for sometimes ignoble, exploitive acts. As Joseph Cropsey has noted, liberal regimes have tended to act as if private conduct affecting the public realm either will be miraculously guided by a standard of the good or will be good merely because free. [20] Constrained by its relatively negative view of the public realm liberalism has not been very effective at constructing a public vision of the good that would provide moral standards directed to the conservation of the regime.

Liberalism developed the idea that the purpose of politics is freedom through security: the safeguarding of interests and the protection of individual right, to the end of allowing each citizen freedom to pursue private satisfaction outside of the public realm. Unlike Marxist thought, liberalism sees the public realm as by nature a play of competing interest, but it does not share the Greek view that the primary purpose of the politician is to resolve conflicts with a view to the shaping of character. Justice is sought, but not in the Platonic sense of the statesman who knows better than the people what is truly due to each, rather in the sense of fairly responding to demands of individuals and groups in order to satisfy the conditions for their private happiness.

Martin Diamond has noted that the liberal idea of natural rights tends to produce a narrowing of the idea of ethics. The politically relevant aspect of morality is reduced to negative prohibitions.[21] And the converse of this tends to be true as well: the ethically relevant aspect of politics becomes the problem of drawing the line beyond which the government cannot extend its authority without oppression.

Yet the ethical aspect of politics in the liberal state has not been insignificant. The commitment to line drawing implies a recognition of the dignity and inviolability of the individual. It rests upon a conviction about the importance to the formation of character of the space necessary to exercise one's abilities without interference. Such a concern is possibly best expressed by Mill in his description of the need to protect the right to be different. Excellence, he argues, can only be developed by each citizen through the cultivation of his nature in the way most appropriate to him. There is an appreciation here of the potential rationality of the individual, his capacity for pursuing his vision of happiness within limits consistent with the opportunity for everyone else to do the same. There is further the sense that when reason is exercised collectively it easily becomes too oppressive and destroys those very qualities of independence and self-reliance which form the basis of worthwhile community life.

Thus the liberal tradition does recognize a connection between the exercise of private freedom that a limited state makes possible and the virtues a people must possess to remain free. The problem remains, however, that liberal theory, as rooted in Hobbes and Locke, does not provide a basis for distinguishing between different levels of ethical merit attaching to the activities men are legally free to pursue. In other words it offers no paradigm for discriminating among character types according to their approach to excellence. Thus Mill in *On Liberty* is intent, not on delineating the character of the good citizen but on establishing the criteria for insuring the citizen's independence of the state. Because for modern liberalism freedom has never been conceived as identical with political life but only as realizable outside of it, the political realm has been viewed as the realm of necessity, to which men are driven by the passion for power and self-preservation. Men enter this realm to secure and protect interests, establish claims, make laws affecting the distribution of necessities—and every law, as Bentham has said, limits someone's freedom to act. But they do not enter the political realm with the idea of encouraging excellence of character in the regime.

The issue of line drawing became more acute for liberal theory in the nineteenth century, for individual freedom had to be reconciled with the problems created by rapid industrialization and a growing demand for equality of conditions, politically and socially. Liberal thinkers began reexamining the question of the responsibility of the state to insure societal welfare. Simple compassion and a new sense of what was fair were part of the motivation for this, but another influence was the already mentioned Enlightenment notion that through the manipulation of institutions a kind of immanent salvation was possible for mankind. Liberal theory began to be influenced by many of the ideas of the "analytical science of man" and to embrace the hope that the ultimate end of achieving a harmonious resolution of society's conflicting goals and desires was possible. In *The New Science of Politics* Eric Voegelin observes that such "an evolution. . .was already anticipated by J. S. Mill's faith in the ultimate advent of communism for mankind."[22]

The dominant trend in liberal theory since Mill has been to draw the line so as to leave very little in society in which government does not feel itself entitled to have a hand. This, on the theory that the complexities of modern life and the know-how of science have made it both necessary and possible for the state to insure the condition for the private satisfaction of all.

I mention private satisfaction, because liberalism has sanctioned the view of the public realm as responsible for securing the needs of the private realm, while retaining the belief that the state's responsibility in this regard is based on utilitarian not ethical ends. That is, liberalism, while succumbing in part to the hope Tocqueville attributes to the French philosophers, of creating a "society in which all [is] simple, uniform, coherent, equitable and rational. . .,"[23] has not accepted the idea that government should shape character, but rather has championed the idea of equalizing and harmonizing the conditions under which the pursuit of private ends takes place.

However, these apocalyptic and materialistic strains in liberal thought have made it vulnerable to the charge that it is merely an inconsistent form of socialism, without socialism's moral vision. Thus, Michael Walzer argues that the process "by which the welfare state extends its sway, cuts individuals loose, isolates them from communal ties, drives them into a material and then an emotional dependency on the central authorities."[24] And Robert Heilbroner has written in *Dissent* that the liberal welfare state is rooted in contradiction because it has tried to undo the anarchy of capitalism without touching the private capital responsible for that anarchy, and "to undo the excessess of bourgeois culture without touching the acquisitive, privatized ethos inseparable from capitalist economic institutions."[25]

Socialist thinkers have pointed to the same issue that Walter Lippmann has raised: the spiritual decay of the Western liberal democracies, which has manifested itself in the decline of their public philosophies. I have argued that liberalism originally had no philosophy of the public realm—other than the negative one of not interfering with individual rights. Welfare state liberalism did not essentially change this. It merely discovered that what previously had been considered interference, was no longer, because modern conditions had shrunk what could properly be considered the private realm.

Lacking a true philosophy of politics, liberalism has been sustained by two things: the universal acceptance of standards of political morality in the early liberal societies, on the basis of a common vision of and commitment to the public good, out of which a public philosophy naturally emerged; and secondly, efforts by statesmen to revive the public philosophy at moments of crisis. The ethos has partly decayed and as Herbert Storing has said, the statesmen have been hampered by not having a theory of statesmanship to guide them.[26] Partly for this reason liberal statesmen and the liberal state have been unable to continue to deal effectively with new forces that have posed a threat to the very character of liberal regimes, such as the desire for absolute equality, the belief in the application of science to political things, changes in the character and impact of economic institutions and the influence of utopian ideology.

Contemporary liberal theorists have for the most part not addressed this problem, either having succumbed to the Marxist vision of a malleable and therefore perfectible human nature or having embraced John Rawls' attempt to use the symbol of the social contract to establish the idea that a regime's legitimacy rests primarily upon the degree of economic equality to which it is committed. Rawls' use of the contract symbolism to demonstrate the justice of economic equality is fraught with the same inadequacies as was its original use by Locke to insure individual freedom. Both are concerned to establish a legal conception of justice dealing with the possession and distribution of things. However, largely as a consequence of this approach, both remain agnostic about the relationship between the basic rules or principles of the regime and the ethical consequences for the regime of the social and political arrangements implied by those principles.

It is the reliance on the contract idea, it seems to me, which forms one of the major obstacles in the way of liberalism developing an idea of politics as concerned with the character of the regime; and of the politician, not as a servant or administrator, but as a leader capable of exercising the prudence necessary for "managing. . .the affairs of the community in deed and speech,"[27] with a view to preserving and enhancing right order in society.

Burke attacked the contract symbolism because of his insight that to base the union of individuals in a state on contract was to replace the bond of community with that of the arbitrary will and opinion of individuals. He believed this had the effect of turning the state away from a concern for shaping character to the more servile task of reflecting the wills of many solitary bearers of contractual rights.

Moreover, Plato, in his analysis of the social contract idea in *The Republic,* argues that it is based on a notion of justice as a compromise between what men desire most—to do injustice with impunity—and what they fear most—to suffer injustice without the ability to retaliate. Justice, then, is seen as a creation or convention of man, a bargain, in a sense, that he makes with the worst part of his nature. This view denies that there can be a true natural justice intrinsic to human relations, complete knowledge of which would allow one accurately to say what is due to each member of society. And what is due to each, in his latter view, means, ultimately, what is best for the soul of each, and thus what ennobles the spirit and elevates the character of a people.

Behind the question of the validity of the social contract symbolism is the question whether society is a product of nature or of convention. This is obviously not a simple dichotomy, since the Greeks recognized that political life was a convention by which man lifted himself above the necessity and force of sheer nature. The basic issue is whether political conventions are seen as fulfilling man's nature or as merely holding it in check. In the latter view society and politics are conceived as artifices that prevent man's natural self from bursting forth. They constitute a compromise between man's self-interest and his desire for self-preservation. Consequently, politics comes to be seen as having the primary purpose of preserving the conditions upon which the original compromise is based. And since it is inevitably based upon considerations of utility, politics must concern itself with reconciling the competing "utilities" of the multitude of partners to the contract. Politics becomes their means of protecting themselves from one another in order to better satisfy private needs.

The Greeks certainly don't reject this as one important purpose of political life. Plato, in *The Republic,* portrays primitive societies as forming because individuals cannot satisfy all their own needs in isolation. Each person's self-interest brings him to seek to share with others. A primitive division of labor forms to meet basic physical needs. Thus society is recognized as having the purpose of satisfying individual interest. But this proves too limiting and the discussion in the *Republic* turns to the problem of organizing society to meet the needs of the spirit as well as those of the body. Plato argues that it is through conventions represented by social and political institutions that man explores on an intellectual level the proper task for each in the division of labor of the spirit that corresponds to that originally attained on the physical level in the first simple exchange society.

The search for the proper division of labor at the level of spirit is the search for justice. And this, although approached through the conventions represented by laws and edicts, customs, habits, and traditions, is the fulfillment of human nature and therefore eminently "natural" for man. For it is through these conventions that communities of men persuade one another about the good they ought to pursue. And it is through constituting communities that seek a good beyond the aggregation of individual utilities that men are able to realize their humanity.

By contrast the contract symbolism leads to a denial of man's potential as a political being, as a communal being capable of reasoning and communicating with his fellows about the ends proper to them all. It precludes a view of politics as, in part, an end in itself, through participation in which virtues are exercised and formed, and expression is given to the highest purposes of the community. The social contract does not give rise to society, rather society gives rise to contract. For only through experience of the possibilities of community do men come to give reasoned assent to the ends they wish it to embody.

In modern commercial republics it is inevitable that the politician will devote much of his time to regulating and balancing competing interests, but unless the political culture, which ultimately takes its guidance from political philosophy, encourages him to perform this task with an eye to the effects of laws and policies on the character of the regime, then the political realm can attain to "utility—but never dignity,"[28] It is especially necessary in democratic republics, with their "incessant jarring of interests. . ."[29] in pursuit of material gain, that politics go beyond the role of referee and concern itself with what Tocqueville calls the "deeper combinations of intellect,"[30] whose exercise ennobles the spirit and elevates the character of a nation. When the political realm takes this as its highest end, government's ultimate task must be to present a vision of the good society and to debate what the true criteria are for judging policies designed to realize that vision.

At bottom this view forces the explicit recognition that every political decision is an ethical decision. It is based on the idea that "political reason looks for. . .the means of adding and subtracting, multiplying and dividing true moral denominations viewed not in a mathematical or metaphysical but in a social and political context."[31] It thus asserts that politics ultimately has to do not with utility-maximizing rules but with the conditions that will promote the emergence of "the better angels of our nature."

The Western political tradition from Plato and Aristotle to modern liberalism is anchored in the recognition that there is an inherent and therefore irreconcilable tension in human existence between the imperfections of man's nature and his need to explore and understand the limits of those imperfections. The denial by utopian thought that a tension is intrinsic to man's nature has led to tragic attempts to go beyond the good society, aimed at by the just use of political reason, to the perfect society, in which all men are promised the temporal salvation of total self-fulfillment. This vision of an ultimate escape from the limitations of man's nature is purchased at the enormous cost of sacrificing the true source of man's dignity—his freedom to reason about the universally valid questions regarding what way of life is possible and proper for him.

If liberal thinkers are to reassert the moral vision implicit in the commitment to individual freedom, they must draw on the Greek teaching that politics is at bottom an ethical enterprise whose ultimate concern is the character of the people. This teaching reminds us that the structure of liberties in liberal-democratic societies does not finally depend on legally codified rights, but on the "moral order in society," an order that both shapes and is shaped by the vision philosophers and statesmen provide of the meaning and purpose of a nation's existence.

# CHAPTER FOUR
# LOCKE AND AMERICAN VALUES
## Robert A. Strong

The United States, it is frequently asserted, is a Lockean regime. The founders were either careful students of the *Two Treatises of Government,* or descendents of a Whig political tradition which had its origins in the *Two Treatises* and the Glorious Revolution. The "Life, Liberty and pursuit of Happiness," in the Declaration of Independence is, after all, only a slight variation of the "Life, Liberty, and Estate" which Locke discusses in the Second Treatise. The self-evident truths that "all men are created equal. . .[and] endowed by their Creator with certain unalienable Rights" may not have been self-evident in the seventeenth century, but they were important to Locke and the other political philosophers of that era who were seeking a basis for political order that did not rest on Biblical history or naked power. While all of this justifies the connection between the writings of John Locke and the creation of the American republic, it would be a mistake to think that the United States is completely a Lockean regime. It would even be a mistake to think that the character of a Lockean regime would be easy to describe.

In Locke's most important political work, the *Two Treatises of Government,* there is no account of what the ideal or the most practical regime would be like. The first Treatise is a critique of Filmer's thesis that the origins of political power can be found in Adam's dominion over the world and subsequently through his descendants, and the Second Treatise presents an alternative thesis finding the origins of political power in consent. In a sense all regimes are Lockean, if Locke is correct about the conditions of man in the state of nature and the way in which political societies evolve. But the Second Treatise is more than an exercise in speculative political anthropology. Locke's account of the development of political society tells us a great deal about the legitimacy of certain regimes, about the purpose of government, and about the limits of political power. Careful analysis of the Second Treatise should permit us to draw the outlines of a Lockean constitution and to compare it with our own. Understanding the fundamental principles and basic institutions of Lockean politics should allow us to judge the extent to which we are a Lockean regime. More importantly, understanding Locke may suggest something about the values which are at the root of American political thought and which account for both the strengths and weaknesses of the American constitutional order.

For Locke government—civil or political society—has a single fundamental purpose, the protection of property.[1] By property Locke means "Life, Liberty, and Estate."[2] Prior to the existence of civil society each individual, having perfect freedom, could take any action necessary to protect his own property. In forming or joining political society, individuals surrender a portion of their freedom in return for government's superior ability to provide protection.

Locke's broad definition of property including life, liberty, and estate can really be narrowed to estate when considering the purpose of government.[3] Liberty in the state of nature is perfect and a voluntary reduction of liberty is involved in the formation of political society. Life in Locke's state of nature is not constantly endangered as it is in a Hobbesean state of nature, and although each individual has the right to punish breaches of the natural law "as he is persuaded the Offence deserves, even with Death it self," these breaches are most likely to arise in disputes over material possessions.[4] Knowing why private material possessions are legitimate and why they need to be preserved is crucial for understanding the ends of a Lockean regime.

Private property is legitimate for Locke because, to the extent that it is useful, property is almost entirely the product of human labor. Since each individual has an absolute property of his own person, he is entitled to keep for himself the goods he produces. Property, particularly land, has value as a result of human activity. Cultivation is responsible for a thousand fold increase in the productivity of land. Although an individual in the state of nature cannot have property in things he will never use (i.e. in food that will spoil in his possession) property is not fundamentally legitimate because of needs. If a man gathers fruits from the forest, they become his property because he has added his labor to them. He may gorge himself in their consumption or convert them into alcohol, and although these uses may not be the most likely ones in Locke's description of primitive human existence, they are not illegitimate. There is nothing in Locke to prevent men from using property to satisfy whims or vices. Property is the product of human activity, but the motivation for that activity is not decisive. Presumably, needs for food, shelter, and clothing would be important motivations for men to labor in the state of nature, but they are not the only ones. Locke suggests that acquisitiveness is the politically crucial motivation. Men in the state of nature are not satisfied with the fact that most natural goods perish. Even if the state of nature is abundant and satisfies all of man's basic needs, he will nevertheless invent money to give lasting value to the perishable goods he produces in excess of his needs. The invention of money involves tacit consent among men that gold and silver will have a permanent value and this consent takes place before any compact forming government. The invention of money makes possible an inequality of private possessions which leads to serious problems in preserving property and eventually to the formation of political society.

Political society does not create property or make it legitimate; it is not even necessary for the invention of money which makes the accumulation of significant amounts of property possible. Political society merely corrects some of the inconveniences in the state of nature that make property difficult to preserve. These inconveniences arise because no effective law or law enforcement exists in the state of nature. The fact that there is a single natural law should logically produce a universal community in which all men live in harmony. It does not and Locke gives us two explanations for why it does not: "the corruption and vitiousness of degenerate Men" who violate the natural laws and the fact that each man is his own judge of when violations occur.[5] Problems can therefore occur either from conscious attempts to steal the property of others (which presumably is more likely when the distribution of property becomes significantly unequal after the invention of money) or from honest disputes where both parties believing themselves to be in the right have no independent authority to which they can appeal. Although the natural law provides an absolute standard, it does not create a harmonious society because men do not obey it or cannot agree on its application. Political society arises to address these problems.

In Locke's formulation of the origins of property and the problems that lead to political society, he differs radically from both Filmer and Hobbes. Property is pre-political and has an existence and justification that does not depend simply on consent. Civil society protects property, which is an important function, but it does not create it; government gives very little to the individual beyond protection of what the individual acquires for himself. This is a radical reduction of the role of government especially when it is contrasted, as it is in the *Two Treatises,* with Filmer's position. For Filmer the origins of political power are a combination of divine providence and parental authority. By associating the will of God and the responsibility of parenthood with the purposes of civil society, the role of government is much more extensive for Filmer than it could ever be for Locke.

Even for Hobbes who rejected the divine right of kings, Locke's description of the purpose of civil society significantly reduces the authority of government. According to Hobbes, entering civil society provided the essential benefit of protection from violent death and therefore the activities of government—taxation, conscription, punishment—even if they became oppressive would always be preferable to the dangers of the state of nature. Locke's state of nature is not mortally dangerous, it is practically inconvenient and the politically relevent human characteristic is not fear of violent death, but acquisitiveness. For Filmer the ruler acts as the descendant of Adam, and all of his actions have a divine sanction. For Hobbes the ruler rescues the individual from the mortal dangers of the state of nature and commands his obedience in all instances (except cooperation in his own execution). For Locke government provides a common powerful and independent authority for settling disputes over property that cannot be settled before the creation of political society. Locke's government gives much less to its citizens, has a weaker command of men's loyalty, and presumably a much more limited scope of activity. Curiously as Locke describes the legislative and executive powers that will be exercised by government, they do not appear to be very limited at all.

Creation of the legislative power is the first and fundamental act of consent in the formation of political society. The first duty of the legislature is to preserve the society. It will also make positive laws for the regulation and preservation of property and it will take such action as is necessary for the public good. Locke devotes an entire chapter to the extent of the legislative power, but the limitations on the legislative power he lists are to a large degree procedural rather than substantive. Laws must be standing and administered by known judges. The power to make laws cannot be transferred and taxes cannot be levied without consent. Finally laws must have as their end the good of the public.

That laws must be standing and fairly adjudicated is a response to the inconveniences in the state of nature that arise when each man acts as his own judge. But the fact that laws must be stated and judged fairly says nothing about their content. Nor does the prohibition against transferring the legislative power prohibit how that power may be exercised so long as it remains in legitimate hands. The requirement that the legislature obtain the consent of the people before taking away their property is a more substantial limitation. It means that the legislature must remain sufficiently representative to satisfy the requirement of consent if it is to levy taxes. Locke states this requirement in an extreme and revealing way when he points out that a "serjeant" may command a soldier to "march up to the mouth of a Cannon," but may not take a single farthing from his pocket.⁶ The significance of this example may not be what it says about the sacredness of property, but what it indicates about the power of government which can command the lives of citizens. If lives must be lost in the defense of the community, then the legislature acting to preserve the society has the right to demand them.

The question of the public good is the most difficult of the legislative limitations to deal with. It is first of all difficult to know what the content of a Lockean public good would be. In the Second Treatise Locke's public good is really the condition which permits the enjoyment of private goods. Political society is formed to settle disputes among men that are difficult to settle in the state of nature which lacks a common and independent judge. But the good that society produces is not the peace that results from an orderly settlement of dispute, but the enjoyment of the things being disputed. Thus the public good would seem to be merely maximization of the enjoyment of property. So in effect the public good is another way of saying "preservation of property" and as such it is a restatement of the ends of civil society without adding much in the way of specific limitations on the action of the legislature. The legislative power can do anything to advance the ends of civil society so long as it does not transfer its authority, obtains consent for taxation, and acts with procedural care through standing laws and known judges. The executive is not even limited by these kinds of procedural considerations.

The executive power in the Second Treatise is extensive because of Locke's description of prerogative. To some extent prerogative is inherent in the executive function. Some executive responsibilities, particularly those involved with foreign affairs will not be guided by law. In domestic affairs decisions may have to be made while those who exercise the legislative power are unavailable. Additionally, laws will always be imperfect because they cannot anticipate all situations or easily specify exceptions. The application of general laws to specific cases, especially the granting of leniency, will always involve prerogative. But Locke's prerogative is much more extensive than the instances of discretion inherent in the executive function. Lockean prerogative may involve violating the law, not just bending it. Locke's definition of tyranny is often quoted, "wherever law ends, Tyranny begins."⁷ But there is an important qualification that is only found in a fuller quotation of that passage, "wherever law ends, Tyranny begins, if the law be transgressed to another's harm." Tyranny is not violation of law, but violation that results in harm. Violating the law with good results is prerogative. So extensive is this power that Locke suggests that the executive may alter the make up of the legislature, which is to say he may violate the fundamental law of the society, to correct inequities in representation that might develop over time.[8] "Prerogative is nothing but the Power of doing publick good without a Rule," and the test of whether prerogative is justified is the public good.[9] ". . .If there comes to be a question between the Executive Power and the People, about a thing claimed as a Prerogative, the tendency of the exercise of such Prerogative to the good or hurt of the People, will easily decide the Question."[10]

The purely Lockean regime consistent with the principles of the *Two Treatises* would be a government based on consent with the limited purpose of protecting property but very broad and indefinite powers. In attempting to apply these principles to describe the purely Lockean regime, the first question we may ask is whether we can determine what form of government such a regime would have. There is, however, almost no mention of forms of government in the *Two Treatises*. In a sense Locke reduces all government to a single form. He eliminates, by definition, all the corrupt or perverted forms that were described in classical political thought. Government is a compact with limited ends and any government that does not serve those ends is either a conquered territory where the inhabitants are slaves or a legitimate government that has dissolved itself as a result of its failure to meet the ends of the compact. If such governments are not overthrown by the people, they continue to exist, not as political societies, but as regions characterized by a constant state of war between the people and the illegitimate rulers. With the perverted forms of government eliminated and all civil societies based on consent, it might be possible to say that for Locke all government is popular government and the question of form is irrelevant. But such a conclusion, even if it is justified, does not tell us much about the institutional arrangements of the purely Lockean regime. Does it follow from the fact that all governments have their origins in an act of consent that the ideal form of government is democratic or republican? Perhaps not. If we look more closely at Locke's treatment of consent, we find that it is by no means clear that the majority who create political society should also run it.

Although Locke specifies that after political society has been formed, the consent of the people will have to be obtained before their property can be taken from them, he does not specify the necessity for seeking consent of the people for other actions. The importance of consent for taxation is not that the people are the best rulers, but that rulers will always want to deprive people of their property. Rulers will be subject to the avarice and ambition that were part of the problem in the state of nature—the motivations to steal property. The requirement for consent before taxation is more a necessary check on the governors than evidence of faith in the governed. The American protest against taxation by Parliament was based on the argument that taxation was an exceptional power. The taxes levied on the colonies may have been small and justified by the expenses of colonial defense, but the power to tax was the power to destroy and the American presumption was that if these taxes did not destroy the colonies others surely would. Locke would agree with such a presumption.

In some sense, therefore, the requirement for consent before taxation is the exception rather than the rule. The legislature and the executive have broad powers and although they are required to act in accordance with the public good, the public good is not specified by prior consent. There are several reasons why Locke does not require prior consent for most actions of government.

First, consent is not the absolute standard for Locke. The natural law has a higher status and the formulation of positive law is a substitute for the natural law. As we know, part of the reason disputes arise in the state of nature is that men can disagree about the meaning or application of the natural law. Men understand the natural law to differing degrees. Locke surely thought he understood natural law better than his readers, and certainly better than Filmer. It is not impossible to imagine Locke granting that a superior understanding of the natural law would make some men better rulers than others.

Second, the people cannot be consulted in all matters of government because they are not completely rational. The people in the Lockean scheme usually take political action, not as an exercise of collective reason, but as the consequence of being harmed. In describing how men will know that a ruler has become absolute Locke points out that "whatever flatterers may talk to amuze Peoples Understandings, it hinders not Men, from feeling."[11] In judging whether or not prerogative is exercised for the public good "the tendency of the exercise of such Prerogative to the good or hurt of the People will easily decide the Question."[12] The decision is made by waiting until action has been taken and measuring the "good or hurt" that is felt by the people. Likewise the "right of revolution" in Locke can only be exercised after a government has so abused its trust that it is dissolved. What is interesting about Locke's statement that "the people shall be judge" of when government has exceeded its trust is not that they are the ultimate authority, but that their authority will be exercised only when the abuses have been so great or so long standing that the judgment is very clear.

Consent, therefore, creates political society, but partly because men's understanding of the higher standard—the natural law—is imperfect. Consent must be obtained to levy taxes, but largely because rulers will abuse the power of taxation without such a strong check. Consent will be the ultimate test of when government exceeds its authority, but only because the abuses will be clearly known in terms of the suffering of the people. Although consent plays a central role in these three respects, it is also clear in the Second Treatise that a Lockean regime could contain institutions which would seem undemocratic by American standards.

Instead of a detailed constitution, the Lockean regime would have a simple compact establishing the legislative and executive powers, but leaving both with broad discretion to act in the public good. The extent of prerogative would be particularly shocking to Americans who have, in recent decades, developed a heightened sensitivity to the dangers of imperial presidents. The Lockean justification for this extensive prerogative and for the broad powers accorded for the legislature comes from a limited respect for the capacity of men for self government. People will know when they have been harmed and when they have suffered for a long time. They will also know, or be expected to know, when taxation is justified. But they will not always, or even usually, know what actions need to be taken to protect society or promote the common good. The only check on government, beyond the restricted taxing power, would be the ultimate check of revolution which could only rarely be exercised. A Lockean regime would be a government for the people, but not necessarily a government of the people or by the people. It would be a government having a limited purpose—the protection of property—but not necessarily a limited set of powers.

In a sense, the United States suffers from the fact that it is a Lockean regime and from the fact that it is not fully a Lockean regime. Ours is a government with both limited purposes and limited powers. We are followers of Locke to the extent that we define our purpose as the maximization of personal liberty and the pursuit of happiness. But are we justified in making our common goal the greatest possible satisfaction of individual desires? Is a public good that gives acquisitiveness free reign a sufficient, or desirable, end for society? Can we build a decent and cohesive society out of the recognition that without law and its enforcement we would degenerate into thieves and quarrelers? These questions about American values need to be asked in light of our Lockean roots.

But another set of questions also need to be asked. Are we insufficiently Lockean? Have we been so concerned about individual liberty and self-government that we have created institutions unable to act in emergencies or in new situations? Have we limited the powers of government to the point where it may not always be able to provide for our common protection? Have we become so afraid of prerogative that we no longer recognize the need for presidential power?

An American reading Locke is forced to think seriously about both the power and the purpose of government. And that exercise, regardless of its outcome, enriches our understanding of the values at the core of our political tradition.

# CHAPTER FIVE
# POLITICAL THEORY, AMERICAN VALUES
# AND FOREIGN POLICY
## Kenneth W. Thompson

Some may question the focus on political theory and tradition in a treatise on American values and the world. Throughout history, however, men have thought about values in the most fundamental way in political thought that endures. Whatever modern social scientists may claim concerning novel approaches to studies of values, the most permanent body of thought we possess on social and political values is that of political theory. Moreover, American thought is part of a broader tradition, that of western political thought inherited by the founders. Indeed, no one can understand early American political thought without understanding the rich legacy from which it is derived. It is impossible, therefore, to discuss American political values without reference to the great political traditions. This is as true of certain fundamental issues, such as the relationship of ethics to politics, as it is of the overall question of the relation of American thought to the history of political thought.

No issue is more fundamental in political theory than that of the relationship between ethics and politics. Not surprisingly, the debate has resumed in discussions by contemporary thinkers of politics and international politics. Is politics a branch of ethics or is ethics an aspect of politics and foreign policy, as Mr. Cyrus Vance declared in an interview in late 1976 on his appointment as Secretary of State?

The wellsprings of American and western thought on ethics and politics are Judeo-Christian, classical, and modern political philosophy. The great merit of Christian thought for international politics was its linking of the vision of the universal brotherhood of man deriving from mankind's common ancestry with the Christian view of man as being both good and evil. Individual Jewish and

Christian thinkers have tended to emphasize one or the other sides of Judeo-Christian thought, the idea of brotherhood or the idea of man's imperfectibility. Both are recurrent themes in tension with one another and neither has been set aside. The message of Christian thought for Americans who seek to interpret American values to the world, therefore, is that because all men are God's children the American dream has relevance for others, but because Americans have shaped that dream with selfishness as much as with vision, it has at best limited relevance. The Christian perspective, therefore, helps men to understand the dilemmas which confront groups and nations in relating ethics and politics. The great merit of classical political philosophy derives from its emphasis on reason and virtue. While acknowledging the limitations of imperfect man, it places stress on the possibilities of relating ethics and politics. Political philosophy has the responsibility of throwing light on what is good, better and best in politics. It is not enough to point the finger at imperfect and sinful man. The philosopher, who enjoys man's highest possibility of political contemplation, must reflect on what is "simply good" and what is good or best under the circumstances. Christian thought falls prey, according to classical philosophers, of overemphasizing the difficulties and ambiguities of politics. The good man who seeks what is good in politics is more likely to realize the good regime. A good regime finds a way of bringing together good men. Individual and collective virtue are related. Man has the ability through reason to achieve good government. His task is not only to perceive the limitations of politics but also its possibilities for good. Moreover, because man is a social animal he realizes his highest potential through participating in politics. Politics in the final analysis is part of ethics.

Christian thinkers in the tradition of Aquinas and some Jewish philosophers with a passion for justice seek to appropriate and adapt classical thought. In so doing, they and classical political philosophers run the risk of casting political virtue in abstract moral categories. Natural law is tempted to propound fixed moral principles that being rigid may thwart the search for what is right in given political circumstances. (The most noteworthy example is the absolute view of birth control and abortion which can clash with social and economic realities and lead to injustice in particular cultures.)

The great merit of modern political philosophy has been to concentrate on the actual conditions of political life. Whereas Christian and classical thought both helped men to understand the ends of politics, modern political thought, in centering on means and excluding the transcendent realm, has focused attention on the social and political order. Of all the great political traditions, it has had most to say about contemporary political arrangements. Its contributions have been noteworthy in providing guides to political action. Its failures are most striking in the breakdown of its prescriptions for the good political society and improved systems of governance. Modern political thought too readily assumes that civilization is on the march, that strengthening one institution of government or another guarantees progress, and that earlier political traditions are irrelevant to contemporary life. Its tendency has been to select out from a multitude of urgent social needs a particular reform promising utopia. In the nineteenth and early twentieth centuries, prison reform, free trade or the long ballot were social and political reforms heralded as announcing the dawn of a new era. In the 1980s, tax reform and military preparedness are being offered as panaceas to all the disorders of national and international life. Some seek the good society through an expansion of executive power and others through its contraction. By singling out some plausible and defensible reform and offering it as the one route to a new and better world, modern political thinkers become ideologues rather than philosophers. They depart from the ancient vision of political contemplation as the highest order of human life.

## A. Three Traditions and Nationalism

Each of the great political traditions has its own conception of human values and the good life. For the Christian, belief in God and serving one's fellow man is uppermost in the Christian hierarchy of values. For the disciple of classical political thought, the search for virtue in society is the highest calling. For modern political thinkers, the establishment of the best social and constitutional arrangements within existing societies is the foremost objective. The Christian and the classical traditions depend on certain objective values and standards above and outside the social and political order. Modern political thought depends for the most part on values and standards within society and the political process. The values of the two older traditions are ultimately transcendent while those of modern political thought are immanent. Contemporary exceptions include those political theories for which the earlier traditions have residual importance as with the founding fathers of the American constitutional and political system.

The prospects of all three political traditions have been diminished, however, by certain forces at work within the present day nation state. Christian thought from its beginnings assumed that man necessarily and inevitably lived in two worlds, the city of man and the city of God. The former was the temporary realm of contingencies, imperfection and sin; the latter was the enduring realm of certainty, perfection and the good. The one was realizable here and now, the other in eternity. The social and political order was structured to reflect, partially at least, the reality of the two worlds. The

Christian vision provided for both a horizontal and vertical dimension in human life with men reaching out to one another in the social order and seeking to know God in the spiritual order. Government was the custodian of the social and political order and citizens were enjoined to give to Caesar what was Caesar's. The church was the custodian of the spiritual order and believers were enjoined to serve God with what was God's.

The rise of the modern nation state and the breakdown of the Corpus Christianum diminished if not destroyed the vision of the two cities. The authority of the one universal church was undermined by the Reformation and the Renaissance. The religion of the prince within emerging political societies determined the religion of the people. Religion and patriotism tended to reenforce one another whereas they had earlier constituted a system of checks and balances interacting with one another. If the universal Catholic Church was in part responsible for the union because of its tendency to equate and make itself co-extensive with the city of God, the embryonic nation state was also responsible by becoming the repository of individual and group morality in order to assure political cohesion. Whereas the church had taught believers the commandment "Thou shalt not kill," princes and rulers taught "Thou shalt kill to preserve the nation state."

Moreover, other forces were at work weakening the hold of the Christian tradition. The Christian tradition in its historical formulation presupposed a world of sheep and shepherd. The modern era has witnessed the growth of ever more complex societies in which the individual to whom Christianity ministered was further and further removed from primary human relations with his fellow men. The great society supplanted the good Samaritan. Furthermore, Christianity itself became more and more fragmented. In America, a great Civil War found men praying to the same God and justifying their acts from the same scriptures. During the conflict, President Abraham Lincoln wrote that "each party claims to act in accordance with the will of God. Both *may* be, and one *must* be wrong. God can not be *for,* and *against* the same thing at the same time." In recent days, Martin Luther King and Jerry Falwell invoke the scriptures to defend actions affecting millions of people in diametrically opposite ways. Maintaining a universal Christian tradition is complicated by the rise of sovereign nation states. "The nation fills the minds and hearts of men everywhere with particular experiences and, derived from them, with particular concepts of political philosophy, particular standards of political morality, and particular goals of political action."[1]

If the Christian tradition has been challenged by the circumstances surrounding the modern nation state, the classical tradition is threatened in a similar way. Modernity has brought about a shift, it is argued, from discussions of the good man and the good state to discourse on political power and political tactics. Classical political philosophy was not unaware of the realities of good and evil in human nature. The Platonic dialogues are filled with examples of cynical and selfish men overriding reason and virtue in their political attitudes and conduct. Yet for the philosopher, contemplating the human drama as a whole, reason was superior to the traditional and virtue was the standard by which cynicism and selfishness were judged. Man approached his true and best nature in participating in the social and political order. He realized himself as a social animal.

However, classicists maintained that man's fulfillment was most attainable within the polity, a small-sized political community in which face-to-face political discourse occurred. By contrast, the citizen in the larger nation states has little if any contact with his rulers. He is remote from the scene of urgent problems and unable to comprehend the complex issues on which he must decide. The closest aide to President Lyndon B. Johnson recently observed that nuclear questions escaped him no matter how faithfully he studied. He was thrown back on finding scientists he could trust. Comprehension required scientific and technical knowledge which only scientific specialists possessed.

The history of modern times throws a cloud over the case that classicists make for reason and virtue. Wise students of political history such as Reinhold Niebuhr, Herbert Butterfield and Hans J. Morgenthau have traced the influence of the irrational in politics. The German people, whose culture matched any in Europe, followed a fanatical leader, Hitler, who stirred popular emotions with slogans of a superior German race. Legislative assemblies, intended for prudent deliberation, become the scene of chauvinist and bellicose debate. National self-determination which promised satisfaction and peace to the world's people was successfully invoked by Hitler for the annexation of the Sudetenland. Reason proved defective in anticipating the consequences of thousands of apparently reasonable acts. Unintended and unforeseen consequences of *reasonable* historical acts outweighed the expected or intended results. Thus the Protestant Reformation, which rested on the proposition that individuals should be free to read and interpret the Bible, weakened individualism to the extent nationalism became all-powerful. The French Revolution which promised liberty, equality and fraternity led to the enlistment of individual Frenchmen in the Napoleonic Empire.

To recite a litany of individual virtues when individuals are swallowed up in big government, big labor or big management seems less relevant in the modern world. More germane are discussions of the problems of hard-pressed individuals seeking to reconcile competing virtues. The busy executive, for whom long hours and neglect of family are sometimes required to assure profits and livelihood, struggles to be a good father. For the devoted parent, caring for children may necessitate overlooking his own parents. Being a man of virtue and principle may not be enough under these circumstances. The truly virtuous man has to find his way through a maze of conflicting principles.

If Christian and classical thought are criticized for too much opposition to modernity and too great a faith in historical political values, modern political thought links modernity with progress. Whereas the older traditions stand in opposition to present trends, modern political theory tends to sanctify them. It glorifies the state and more particularly certain branches of government favored one after the other as the cycle turns. Transposed to the international scene, modern thought manifests an exaggerated confidence in institutions as instruments for transforming international realities. It has viewed the United Nations, the World Bank and the U.N. Specialized Agencies as answers to all the difficult problems of international politics. The rise and fall of popular enthusiasm for each of these institutions in turn has thrown into question the judgment of modern thought. It has also led some contemporary thinkers to reopen the question of the relevance of Christian and classical thought to present day problems.

Those who are dissatisfied with modern approaches to political values may not acknowledge the need to reexamine the meaning of the great political traditions. More often they declare that they offer the world a wholly new or radically reformulated political vision. Thus we the people are offered radicalism, neo-conservatism, pragmatism or moral majoritarianism as though such approaches bore no relationship to intellectual and political debates which have gone on over the centuries. It may be a pecularily American trait to think that no one else has struggled with the classic issues of politics. In order to reach a wide audience, political observers and pundits may have to speak as though they were addressing controversies for the first time. Political scientists most of all are proud to proclaim that their primary endeavor is to make of politics a science not a mere exercise in intellectual history. Their task is not to stir the bones of dead men or breathe life into old ideas. Periodically, they and their heirs offer the world a new political science purged of ancient truths that have lost all salience for modern man.

However the rhetoric of the architects of a new political science often conceals what can be discovered by looking beyond rhetoric. It remains true that virtually every issue in contemporary political science—behavior vs. thought, empiricism, value-free science and tradition vs. change—has been discussed and evaluated within the great political traditions. In truth, "there is nothing new under the sun." For this reason, the examination of the historic debate over values has contemporaneity in the present. The search for truth far from requiring that men bury the past demands reexamination. If it is true, as a leading authority wrote, that we have no present theory of political values in the world, one promising route in the search is reconsidering the efforts of the past.

# B. Four Changes and the Traditions

Not only has the rise of the nation state profoundly affected the relation of the great political traditions to politics but so have the changing patterns of international politics and diplomacy. Historically, the Christian and classical political traditions assumed a consensus on values within the Christian and classical worlds. Four developments have altered the political world within which any of the historic traditions must operate. First, a worldwide system of political ideologies and conflicting religious faiths has replaced the Christian Europe of which historians like Christopher Dawson wrote in tracing the formation of western Christendom. [2] Universal Christendom lost out to a pluralistic international system of competing nation states and cultures. Second, the political faiths which inspired men took on the characteristics of the terrestial world rather than the adornments of the heavenly city. To the extent the latter existed at all it was a "this worldly" utopia. Carl Becker described the heavenly city of the eighteenth century philosophers; Marx and Lenin elaborated a creed that identified the end of history with the Marxist classless society. Salvation was achievable here and now and its standards were not outside but within history. The direct application to international problems of the Christian tradition was undermined by the breakdown of a consensus on values and the disappearance of faith in effective objective moral principles outside history.

Two other developments coincided and reenforced the above mentioned changes. They profoundly affected the relevance of the classical tradition. The first occurred with the vast increase in the size of viable political units. The movement from city states to nation states culminated in the postwar emergence of the superpowers. To speak of good men creating good regimes became a difficult proposition to sustain. Good and bad men alike seized power in large collective states claiming that only they were capable of solving the momentous social problems of great masses of people. Events that good men had prophesied were rationally impossible, such as global depressions, world wars and totalitarianism, followed one another in rapid succession. Large populations responded to programs whose defenders argued that they served all the people. If Americans had any doubts concerning the far-reaching effects of this third development they had only to compare the deliberative processes of leaders addressing the New England town meeting with Mussolini or Hitler haranguing the German and

Italian people with the claim, "forty million Italians (Germans) can't be wrong." In a word, the concept of popular sovereignty replaced that of personal virtue.

A fourth development was the radical transformation of political communication. Classical political thought had maintained that personal and collective morality were indivisible. In the modern era, not only totalitarian rulers but democratic leaders determined what was moral and right not based on their personal morality but on the interests of states. While certain moral principles applicable to individuals survived in the eighteenth century idea of *raison etat,* as Machiavelli had clung to the concept of *virtu,* contemporary rulers maintained that whatever their personal moral standards on war or slavery, national unity and preserving the state took precedence and were controlling. Thus both Christian and classical thought lost a large measure of their force in the face of far-reaching historical changes.

Modern political thought appeared to offer an alternative to the decline of the ancient traditions. Especially liberalism held out the promise to the great mass of the people of human improvement through universal public education. Today's pressing problems would yield to the workings of free society. Individuals, ever more enlightened by science and reason, would throw off human traits and archiac political ideas and institutions that had led throughout history to conflict and war. Individual man pursuing his selfish interests would be guided nationally and internationally as if by a hidden hand to act in the common good. Nationally, the process would operate in free market economies guaranteed to serve the general welfare. ("What is good for General Motors is good for America," a cabinet member in the Eisenhower administration prophesied.) Internationally, Woodrow Wilson proclaimed that national self-determination would lead to a peaceful world never dreaming that Hitler would invoke a Wilsonian principle to justify his expansionist policies. Moreover, national and international economic stagnation in the 1930s led millions of people to turn to new and more dynamic collectivist solutions.

Not only did the four developments sound the death knell of the effectiveness and coherence of the three great political traditions; another factor sped the disintegration of the international political order. The values which had introduced a limited degree of stability within single political communities proved ineffective on the international stage. The standards that had assured relative peace within nations proved ineffectual or largely irrelevant in international affairs. What was disallowed or dealt with as an exception to the normal processes of national societies was accepted as inevitable in international society. While civil war represented the breakdown of the political order within nations, war was accepted as the continuation of diplomacy by other means in relations among nation states.

The problem as Reinhold Niebuhr discussed it in a succession of treatises on foreign policy was that in international politics no single moral principle existed for ordering all other separate moral principles.³ In international politics, rough and ready norms such as "damage limitation" became the overarching principles rather than such benign standards as the quest for the good society or for communities aimed at human self-fulfillment. In the end, modern political thought which had promised a new and better world became an even more tragic victim to history than Christian or classical thought.

## C. Political Theory and the 1980s

For these reasons, the culmination of history on the international stage was not the heavenly city but the nuclear age. The end of warfare which liberal political thinkers had predicted yielded to the spector of warfare as universal human destruction. Ironically, human advancement and progress led not to the refutation of ancient political truths but to their rediscovery. Prudence has once more become the master virtue in international politics at a moment in time when anything less is a threat to human existence. But political prudence was an idea that Aristotle set forth as a guide for political practice as distinct from political contemplation. From Aristotle and Augustine through Edmund Burke to Niebuhr and John Courtney Murray, prudence as an operative political principle was kept alive not as any rigid formulation or precise definition of what was right or wrong but as a concept of practical morality. Leaders embracing prudence are enjoined not to think of what is invariant in human relations but what practical reason may dictate under a given set of circumstances. Practical morality involves the reconciliation of what is morally desirable and politically possible. It offers few absolutes but many practical possibilities. Prudence is the central precept in the ancient tradition of moral reasoning. It recognizes the need for moral man in an immortal world to find his way through "a maze of conflicting moral principles" no one of which reigns supreme.

Thus justice is a moral objective in international politics but so is international peace. Freedom is a value which must compete with national security. In the same way that the Supreme Court within the United States declared that freedom doesn't give men the right to cry fire in a crowded theater, so internationally the establishment of free states everywhere cannot justify the overriding of the necessity for order or survival in the newer and poorer nation states. Resistance to the spread of communism, which is a clear objective of Americans, may clash with the realities of communist societies that are unlikely to change except through the historic processes of nations like China and Yugoslavia that must work their way through to their own "best possible regimes." Indiscriminate anti-communism can no more be equated with political prudence as a coherent foreign policy for Americans than indiscriminate world revolution can for the Soviet Union.

National interest as a guide to foreign policy may at first glance seem remote from the ancient ideas of prudence of Christian and classical writers. Yet what political realism and practical reason have in common is acceptance of the best solution appropriate to particular circumstances. Philosophers and reformers may offer more glittering answers to the world's problems. It is unlikely any other approach can come closer to a practical way of thinking. Every foreign policy decision in the present situation has its military, political and Soviet-American dimension. Too often policymakers chose policies that apply exclusively to one or the other dimension. Prudence requires attention to all three dimensions and an attempt to find best possible solutions after giving weight to all three. Tragically, the political process by which men come to office in the United States is unlikely to produce the capacity to think clearly at once in all three dimensions of foreign policy. Yet anything less will likely lead on to disaster in American foreign policy.

Ethics and foreign policy requires a summoning of the great political traditions and both ancient and modern political wisdom. Foreign policy is doomed if it lacks experimentation and innovation. In equal measure, it demands lessons of the past from political thought as well as history.

# III. CONTEMPORARY PROBLEMS AND AMERICAN VALUES

### CHAPTER SIX
### ON MACHIAVELLI AND VIOLENCE
### Dante Germino

What we find in Machiavelli is not so much a doctrine as an account of violence as a phenomenon. And yet to say that we have an "account" of a "phenomenon" is to make Machiavelli sound dull—which he almost never is. The astonishing quality of Machiavelli's writing is its aliveness, its capacity for evoking the tangible flavor and turmoil of political existence.

Machiavelli lays before his readers the various manifestations of violence: its different shapes, contexts, gradations, and results. He also treats of the moral dilemma in which the employment of political violence places a man of conscience.

Violence in human affairs is a reflection of the violence in nature itself. Nature, we are told both in the *Discourses* and in the *History of Florence,* operates in a similar fashion both as to "simple" and "mixed" bodies: it "purges itself" of "superfluous matter" for the "health of the body." Human societies are mixed bodies. Everything of human generation is periodically destroyed "of necessity" by "disease, famine, or inundation" in order that men "having become few and humble, may live more commodiously and become better." The course decreed by nature (or by "the heavens") is that of birth, growth, and death.[1]

Violence resulting from human agency need not be destructive. In fact, if prudently managed by men of "rare brain," it may be preservative of the best in human life. *"Colui e viol per guastare, non Quello che e per racconciare, si debbe riprendere."*[2] This sentence is difficult to render into English, but it means that the man who uses violence to waste or destroy, not he who uses it to preserve and to mend, ought to be reproved or censured. There is a distinction, then, between constructive and destructive violence in politics.

Constructive political violence is judged by its "result" or "outcome." The "many" or the "common people" *(el vulgo)* are always impressed by the immediate results or the outcome of actions rather than by the intentions of the ruler or rulers or by the manner of devising or executing these actions.[3] The political leader must see matters through the "mirror of the many" or otherwise, like Piero Soderini, he will not maintain himself in power.[4] The many, however, are unreliable judges of the "reality" as distinct from the "appearance" of things. They "see" but do not "touch" things and they are "often" deceived. To concentrate exclusively upon the visible effects of an action may lead one to attribute a successful outcome to a policy which was ill-devised but which chanced to succeed; similarly, good counsels may through the operation of *fortuna* lead at times to bad results.[5]

The true judge of whether political violence has been constructive is not the many but "most excellent men" of "very rare brain." These are the men of *virtu,* including above all the heroic founders of great republics and kingdoms. Violence regularly attends the founding of a new political order, in part because "one man only" must secure himself against rivals for leadership in the enterprise (hence the "necessary" slaying of Remus by Romulus) and because the masses of men are moved more by the tangible, if inadequate or minimal, benefits of the existing order than by promises of a new order which they cannot see.

Violence is "excusable" and "necessary," then, under certain conditions. It is not excusable for founding a tyranny. It is not excusable when the "arts of peace" or astute dissimulation are sufficient to preserve and defend the *patria.* But it is excusable in founding and in periodically refounding a provisionally "just" political order and in expanding that order if circumstances require it. Imperialism, or the subjection of previously independent peoples by violence or by the threat of violence, is excusable if carried out under a republican constitution of a particular type. That such imperialist expansion may even decree the obliteration of a Carthage, another one of the great republics of history, is an irony which Machiavelli remarks upon in the *Discourses.*

Sheldon Wolin has said that Machiavelli offers us an "economy of violence,"[6] but it is difficult to see wherein the "economy" consists. Certainly Machiavelli was personally opposed to random, senseless violence, and his writings on the subject are presumably designed to increase self-conscious, intelligent reflection on the employment of violence by political actors. I agree fully with Wolin that Machiavelli's outlook is not at all congenial with romantic talk of "purification by the holy flame of violence," if indeed this is an accurate rendition of the teaching he attributes to Sorel.[7] Nonetheless, Wolin goes too far in maintaining that Machiavelli devised a "new science" which would make "brutality and cruelty unnecessary."[8] Wolin attributes to the Florentine Secretary the "conviction that the 'new way' could make no greater contribution than to create an economy of violence, a science of the controlled application of force."[9] The masses of men are said to respond well in Machiavelli's eyes to "controlled doses of fear and violence, to the alternating caress of love and hope, thus making brutality and cruelty unnecessary."[10]

Wolin properly notes that Machiavelli refuses to "weave ingenious veils of euphemism to conceal the ugly fact of violence."[11] Yet what is the so-called "new science" of the "controlled use of violence" which eliminates "brutality and cruelty" but another veil of euphemism? And it was not one woven by Machiavelli, who is no think tank intellectual dealing in euphemisms such as "kill ratios," "surgical strikes," and "nuclear war games." Machiavelli never for an instant allows us to forget that it is real, living people who are killed by cruel and brutal means even in so-called "just" and "necessary" wars. (*Prince,* Ch. 26, *History of Florence,* V.)

Take the famous chapter thirty of Book III of the *Discourses,* for example. There the Florentine Secretary is writing about methods of dealing with envy by a great leader and innovator. He notes that in *una citta corrotta, dove la educazione non abbia fatto in loro alcuna bonta,* there is no alternative but to kill those who out of "perversity" and "malignity" of disposition would bring about the "ruin of the *patria.*" Thus a political leader of *virtu,* if fortune does not otherwise bring about the removal or weakening of the evil and envious opponents, will not hesitate to annihilate them all. "And he who reads the *Bible* judiciously *[sensatamente]* will see that Moses was forced. . .to kill an infinite number of men who, moved by nothing but envy, opposed his desires."[12]

By contrast, the difficulty with Piero Soderini was that he did not know that "time waits for no one, goodness is not enough, fortune varies, and malace cannot be placated."

Numerous other examples could be given to show that Machiavelli scarcely anticipates the elimination of cruelty through the "controlled" or "scientific" use of violence. Rather, as in the *Prince,* chapter eight, he distinguishes between cruelties "well-used" and cruelties "badly used, if we may speak well of what is evil." Machiavelli consistently calls a spade a spade, and evil means, even if they are "excused" politically are never justified morally.

There is no way, then, to insure that political violence will be limited, contained, or "surgical." In fact, if the survival of the *patria* is at stake, it is "good to defend it in any way whatsoever."[13]

One of the most dramatic accounts of political violence in the *Discourses* is that respecting the killing by Junius Brutus of his own sons. Far from shrinking from this terrible act, Machiavelli applauds Brutus' "severity" as both "necessary and useful" in "maintaining in Rome the liberty which she had acquired." And the Florentine Secretary grimly notes how the father not only sat in judgment on his sons but witnessed their execution ("a rare example in all the memory of things"). From this, Machiavelli derives the conclusion that "in a change of regime, whether from republic into tyranny or from tryanny into republic, a memorable execution against the enemies of the present condition is necessary. And he who sets up a tyranny and does not kill Brutus, and he who creates a free state and does not kill the sons of Brutus, maintains himself only a brief time."[14]

Thus, Machiavelli sought to present, for the "common benefit of everyone," (*Discourses,* Preface, Book I) an account of politics that stressed not only the economy, but the ubiquity. The manner in which the account was expected to benefit everyone is not clear, however. The Secretary can be read at different levels. It would be foolish to assume after his many references to dissimulation and "hiding" his meaning that it can be found in any literal reading of his work.[15] The shocking examples and counsels are clearly the work of a consumate literary artist who writes to retain our interest and arouse our reflection by being deliberately provocative.

On one level Machiavelli seems to be saying that good men must conquer their scruples about using cruel and violent means. Otherwise the field will be left to the unscrupulous and a regime of liberty *(uno sato libero)* will be a thing of the past. It will be "to the benefit of everyone," then, to make available to men in general, knowledge of the inescapable presence of violence as a part of political life so that it will come to be used as often for republican liberty as it has always been employed for tyranny and oppression.

Certainly it seems that Machiavelli is desirous of creating a new consciousness about violence in men. He wants to wipe away illusion and can't by taking a fresh look at the subject. Part of his message seems to stress the ambiguity of violence. Violence of a type may lead to a political good; in fact, violence and political freedom seem often to go together. The turmoil which periodically rent republican Rome as a result of the conflict between the patricians (or, more generally, the *grandi*) and the plebeians was productive o f liberty, while submissiveness and tranquility on the part of the common people could only insure their servitude. The princes of contemporary Italy had allowed their peoples to grow weak and effeminate. Ancient *virtu,* which in Italian hearts is not yet dead, must be rekindled through the creation of citizen militias to replace the mercenaries.

* * * *

Machiavelli is by no means silent about the moral dilemma posed to the good man who uses violence. If we are to take literally a famous sentence from a letter written late in his life to Vettori, Machiavelli posed the conflict as one between love of one's country *(patria)* and love of one's soul *(anima).* The effective political leader and the good republican citizen must be willing to love his country even more than his soul.[16]

How literally are we to take this casual remark? And what ultimately is the *patria* of the man who confessed of a "natural" desire to produce a teaching for the "benefit" of "everyone"? Is it not possible that part of that "benefit" is to lay before mankind in a plain way for all to see the ultimate senselessness and futility of violence as a way of political life? Can the Florentine Secretary, who writes ordinarily from the perspective of what Henri Bergson, in his great work of 1932 *Les deux sources de la morale et de la religion,* described as the "closed society," also be aware, if inadequately and obscurely, of the possibility of man to advance to the creation of an "open society"?

Bergson defines the closed society as one whose "members hold together, caring nothing for the rest of humanity, on the alert for attack or defense, bound, in fact, to a perpetual readiness for battle."[17] The moral attitude of the man with a "closed soul" is that of someone who is "part and parcel of society; he and it are absorbed together in the same task of individual and social preservation. Both are self-centered."[18] There is a radical discontinuity between the closed and open moralities. The former is "natural" and the latter "acquired"; the former is formed in response to "pressure" while the latter represents "aspiration" and moral "liberation"; the former is grounded in the sentiment of "love of mankind."[19] The politics of the closed society is irremediably (and here Bergson sounds very much like Machiavelli) the politics of murder. Murder "has all too often remained the *ratio ultima,* if not *prima,* of politics. An abomination, no doubt, but imputable to nature as much as to man. For nature has at her disposal neither imprisonment nor exile; she knows only the sentence of death."[20] Since all the "instincts of discipline" in the closed society "originally converged towards the war-instinct, we are bound to ask to what extent the primitive instinct can be repressed or circumvented. . ."[21]

It is, perhaps, not idle to advance the hypothesis that in Machiavelli we have, side by side the luminous exposition of the character of closed politics and the possibilities for self-conscious action within it, intimations of a new politics and morality of humanistic openness not dissimilar from that so brilliantly and lucidly expounded by Bergson toward the end of the modern epoch. Bergson speaks of the great religious mystics as the true heroes of humanity. And while the florentine Secretary does not so often or so profoundly speak of them, it is true that in *Discourses* I, 10, he lists founders of religion ahead of founders of republics or kingdoms as most praised among men. The tension between the open and closed soul is dramatically revealed in *Discourses* I, 26, where the ruthless means of Philip of Macedon are described as "exceedingly cruel" and "repugnant to any community" of men, let alone to one that calls itself Christian. It were better that every man should live as a private citizen than as a king with such destruction of men to his credit.

In his perceptive Introduction to the recent re-issue of Walker's translation of the *Discourses,* Bernard Crick, following Isaiah Berlin, maintains that Machiavelli's "terrible originality" consists in his recognition that the two moralities, "the morality of soul and the morality of the city, "are irreducible to each other and that both standards "are at work simultaneously." The Secretary is held implicitly to have challenged" the whole traditional view that moralty must be of one piece." For Crick, Machiavelli discovered an "ultimate incoherence" in our "whole culture—perhaps in the nature of things." [22]

There is much to be said for this interpretation. It is perhaps also true, however, that the possibility for overcoming this very duality by human intelligence and will envisioned in the great Florentine's writings. For Machiavelli was not fatalist, and if not a forerunner of the Enlightenment, he did repeatedly profess confidence in man's capacity to chart a new way and to arrive at a new knowledge for the relief of man's estate. For man, although a part of nature was endowed with the capacity to understand and perhaps even, with her aid, to rise above her stern dictates.

# CHAPTER SEVEN
# CODE OF ETHICS AND VALUES
Testimony of Dante Germino before the Select
Committee on Ethics of the United States Senate

Thank you, Mr. Chairman, for your kind invitation to address
this distinguished body. In my judgment, nothing could be more
important than the subject you are considering, because as Plato
and Aristotle demonstrated long ago, politics and ethics go hand in
hand with each other. Politics in the true sense is based on ethics,
which is to say, on a theory of the good life. The heart of political
corruption, therefore, is the substitution of wealth, power, or
prestige for service to the common good. A legislator who uses his
high office for financial gain betrays not only the public trust of
those who have elected him, but all those brave human beings
throughout our history who have risked their lives, their fortunes,
and their sacred honor, that we might live in peace and freedom.

Although, following convention, I have labelled my remarks to
you this afternoon "testimony;" I should emphasize that I do not
conceive it to be my mission to offer specific suggestions for
amending the Senate's Code of Conduct. Rather, I wish to call attention to a significant omission from the Code.

As has been noted, the present Senate Ethics Code is "completely devoid of any substantive discussion of ethics." The
absence of such a discussion can leave only one impression on the
reader: that, in the opinion of the Senate, ethics consists of in-
credibly detailed lists of rules and requirements governing the conflicts of interest, financial disclosure and the like, and that if a
Senator is not in violation of these rules, he or she is acting ethically.

There was a time when ethics was viewed in a radically different
fashion: this was the time of our nation's founding. The purpose of
my remarks is to urge this Committee to take an active role in the

ethical reeducation of the Senate, and as a consequence, of the American people.

In order for this goal of ethical reeducation to be accomplished, I wish to stress the need for exploring our rich tradition of ethical and political thought. That tradition extends beyond the work of the founders themselves to the Athens of Plato and Aristotle. Before we can hope to go forward in ethics, we must recover, as T. S. Eliot said, what has been lost.

What is there to recover? Quite simply, there is an affirmative vision of the full, developed life to be recovered. The heart of ethics is affirmation, not negation. Without public images to move us once again towards giving—giving of ourselves instead of always thinking acquisitively—any legislative set of prohibitions will remain a monument to the malpractices of the age.

In my judgment, today there is no way to recover insight into ethics without a serious study by the legislators themselves of the classics of political theory. What does theory have to do with practice? Everything. Let me now turn to a few brief considerations about the relevance of political theory.

As Aristotle demonstrated in his *Nicomachean Ethics,* a wise decision is the result of a process which begins in the recesses of the mind and heart of the decisionmaker. Aristotle contends that the key virtue of the good legislator is practical reason, which translates the general, theoretical knowledge of that which is good and right (which he calls the "right by nature") into action demanded by a particular situation.

Plato dramatized the relationship between theory, the love of truth for its own sake, and practice in his famous allegory of the cave. The implication of the story Plato has Socrates tell in the *Republic* is that without theory, the legislator will see only the shadows on the wall of the cave, and will mistake them for reality. To "see" the good, one must turn around from the world of everyday desires and walk out of the cave of practice into the sunlight of theory. Then and only then can the legislator, having reentered the cave to serve his fellow citizens, see the goals most widely esteemed in the everyday world—such as love of power, wealth, and prestige—for what they are. Power, wealth, and prestige are not good in themselves; their rewards are transitory and they pale into insignificance in the light of the Good itself.

The legislator who is not theoretically oriented is likely to have as his or her standard of the good only that which is conventional rather than that which is natural. There will be no perspective from which the conventional norms, traditions, and current practices of the society can be critically evaluated. Lacking theory, he will only know what is good by convention (common agreement) rather than what is good by nature.

It is true, as Bernard Lonergan and Eric Voegelin have pointed out, that there is a kind of ethical insight called "common sense," which the best legislators have and which enables them to make many wise decisions without being fully aware of their basis. Acting according to common sense has much to commend it, but it falls short of acting in accordance with theoretically informed practical reason.

Common sense, or the best sense of the community in which one participates, is highly specialized, being the result of customs, traditions, informal agreements, and unspoken rules that have evolved over the years for a particular institution. In the Senate, common sense is presumably the sense of "the Club." Because it is specialized and oriented toward precedent, common sense cannot guide the member of Congress in confronting novel pressures and moral dilemmas emanating from unexpected changes in society. Common sense is bound by precedent, not open to innovation. Common sense can be complacent, and it can accept a moral climate which is unacceptable according to the standard of the right by nature. Common sense confers moral legitimacy on what "everybody does," i.e., everyone in "the Club."

* * * *

## Some Practical Suggestions for the Senate Ethics Committee

In my remaining time, I wish to emphasize the importance of your committee's assuming the leading role in the ethical reeducation of the Senate. Rather than spending your time on how to catch more crooks, I respectfully suggest that you concentrate on how to produce more Senators like the late Frank P. Graham of my home state of North Carolina. Frank Graham was a deeply religious man, but his religiousness was inclusive rather than exclusive. His virtues of humility, frugality, and compassion were immediately evident to everyone who knew him. He inspired allegience and idealism in those who listened attentively to his eloquent speeches. Long before public pressure mounted, he worked to overcome the attitudes supporting racial segregation.

Thomas Jefferson had an abiding faith in the value of ethical education. In founding the University of Virginia, he wanted all its students to become familiar with the "elementary books of public right," by which he meant the classics of political theory from Plato to Locke. No one could attain theoretical literacy without a knowledge of these works, he insisted.

As is well known, today our legislators in general are in a condition of theoretical illiteracy. How many Senators may be seen carrying around one of the "elementary books of public right?" How many Senators make time in their schedule for reflection and discussion about the nature of ethical inquiry?

It may be said that my question is inappropriate to active political life, with all its pressures and time demands. Please consider, however, that the founders of our nation were great readers of the classics, their minds not having been ruined by television and the constant hunger for media exposure. After all, reading a few pages of Plato might spoil the opportunities to appear on prime time!

As I understand it, Mr. Chairman, you and your colleagues are seriously considering the possibility of attaching a "philosophical" preamble to your revision of the present code. I think that this is worth attempting, for in such a preamble you could emphasize that ethics is something more than or even something different from a set of legalistic prohibitions. Instead, ethics is the attempt to shape our lives according to the highest pitch of the reality we experience from within. Ethics implies openness to the ground of our being; it originates in a pre-intellectual orientation toward the Good. To view ethics as a list of legalistic rules, many of which might be avoided on technicalities, makes a travesty of our democracy. Although drafting the language of a preamble which emphasizes these points would be difficult, it is worth attempting. It would be important to avoid sententious moralizing about matters which are not central to the official conduct of the Senators. Rather, the purpose of the preamble should be to evoke a noble vision of their office and of its potentialities for bringing out the best contributions from every human being.

Another proposal to be considered is the organization of seminars to be led by prominent scholars in the humanities. A small group of Senators and selected staff members might read selections from the classics of political theory (such as Plato's *Republic,* Machiavelli's *The Prince* and *Discourses,* Hobbes's *Leviathan,* Locke's *Two Treatises of Government,* and *The Federalist Papers).* Robert Bellah, Irving Kristol, Kenneth Thompson, and other distinguished political and social theorists could be invited to Washington for a period of time ranging from one month to a year to direct such seminars. This program could be modeled after the National Endowment for the Humanities' seminars for professional people. From recent, first-hand experience with such a seminar, I know many professional people (physicians, hospital administrators, lawyers, journalists, etc.) have a hunger for the classics. This should be true also for Senators.

A framework should be erected in which busy people are encouraged to put reading and reflection ahead of every other activity for a period of time. It will be said that the Senators are too busy. Nonsense. It is all a question of priorities. If the case can be made for the relevance of theory to practice, enough Senators will set aside time on their calendars for ethical inquiry inspired by a sustained, directed reading of the classics. These Senators and their staffs could make a profound impression on the ethical climate of the entire Senate.

Our nation's founding was made possible by a commitment to what Walter Lippmann called "public philosophy." Somehow, this public philosophy seems then to have counted more than arms and wealth in guaranteeing America's survival. Nowhere is the relevance of theory to practice more evident than in the effects of the lack of such a public philosophy today. One of the Committee's major tasks might be to look into the character of the American public philosophy and the nature of the current crisis of the spirit in which our country finds itself. By engaging seriously in ethical reflection, the Senate might greatly assist our nation in recovering a sense of transcendent purpose.

Thank you, Mr. Chairman, for this opportunity to appear before your committee. I will be pleased to answer any questions which you or your members may have. I wish you every success in your deliberations, which are important not only to the Senate, but to our country as well.

# CHAPTER EIGHT
# HUMAN RIGHTS AND AMERICAN VALUES
## Kenneth W. Thompson

The spectacle of the rise, fall and rise of human rights on national agendas leads to a search for causes and reasons. Such shifts would be worth passing comment, but not political and philosophical analysis, if national rhetoric or administrative organization for human rights merely reflected the likely and expected turns in national moods and domestic politics. However individual human beings may gain security or suffer shipwreck because of movements on the curve. In human rights, human lives are at stake. Therefore, someone must undertake the task thinkers have pursued for centuries of political theorizing, in this case not on classic themes but about the contemporary subject of human rights. However hazardous or pretentious, the task has importance, no less than worthwhile activist efforts or badly needed case studies. It is not enough to explain all changes in human rights policies by reference to foreign or national crises, changing leadership or social malaise, important as any or all may be. Equally important are the dominant approaches and intellectual trends within and among societies. Three in particular deserve analysis.

## A. Approaches

The first approach which periodically expresses itself in the United States and, I would suppose, in other nations is the tendency to make of human rights or of a given human right an absolute. No nation nor political movement holds a monopoly of this approach. Within most countries, jurists or social and political leaders select out of the rich variety of constitutional or political principles one that ranks supreme. For example, in the United States the distinguished Associate Justice of the Supreme Court, Hugo Black, once argued that either the first amendment of the Constitution on freedom of speech and press was absolute or it was nothing. A long succession of cases decided by the Court showed that his colleagues did not agree. "Free speech," they wrote, "doesn't mean the right to cry fire in a crowded theater." The first amendment has in fact been read in relationship to other values including national security and public order. Given all of life's complexities, it would be surprising if anything else was the case.

Something more is involved here, however, than the process of social and political choice. Moralism, which is *the tendency to subordinate all values to one supreme value,* persists because of what is at stake. Commitment to a single value need not always inspire a crusade. It is one thing to insist within a university, on the priority of the library—a position librarians espouse—without generating a social movement. By contrast, the contagious moral fervor in which large groups are caught up concerning one human right or human rights broadly conceived results from the generality of the moral and political objective. Scholars and students may suffer if librarians fail; all men are threatened if crusaders for human rights fail.

Yet an examination of the basis of moral absolutism as a human rights perspective does not end here. Health as a social objective affects not the one but the many. It too has its generality. I worked for a large private foundation whose early efforts were devoted exclusively to improving the health of the population of nations, notably the rural poor but also the wider population as it was threatened by the ravages of illness and infectious disease. The foundation's early history resounds with declarations by its leaders that no other goal was worth pursuing unless health first was assured. Yet I do not recall in later years or even in the earlier historical documents any evidence that health became a public crusade. The debate went on within the foundation, as it later went on nationally inspired by President Richard M. Nixon's proposals for a vast increase in cancer research or with Senator Edward Kennedy's national health insurance plan. Values competed and objectives were advanced that were weighed in relationship to one another. Latter day foundation leaders found that feeding mankind was at least as supreme a value as preserving health; the debate between Senator Kennedy and Secretary of the Department of Health, Education and Welfare, Joseph Califano, over health insurance found two liberal leaders with a common dedication to the good society arguing not health as an absolute but health vs. solvency. Evidently health as a single objective, compared with human rights as a more general objective, lends itself more readily to pragmatic debate. It also became, as both medical spokesmen in the private foundation world and Senator Kennedy on the national political front learned, a less inspiring and unifying objective than human rights however general its impact on people.

One of the reasons, then, for the appeal of human rights is its ability to arouse political passion. When Thomas Jefferson announced that if he should be required to choose between a government without a free press or a free press without a government, he would choose the latter, he stirred popular emotions. Nothing in the political creed of the Federalists was as closely linked with the sentiments of the populace. Leave aside whether the author of the Louisiana Purchase expressed a working political belief or a captivating political slogan. For the people, Jefferson's placing a free press above government was as credible in his day as President Reagan's putting free enterprise above government in our day, however profound their differences. Both tapped public emotions, galvanized public responses and captured the people's attention. So did President Jimmy Carter when late in the 1976 presidential campaign, and almost by accident, he proposed that human rights be seen as *the* soul of American policy. Political absolutes depend on moral fervor; they require the invocation of something more than rational conviction that a single objective or set of objectives deserve priority. The people must be persuaded, however simply they view political values, that one set of values are historically and morally supreme, not for the moment but for all time. For societies who imagine they are well fed or in good health, food and health are unlikely to become political absolutes. However freedom and well-being may. Not only is their pursuit never exhausted, (not distinguishing them from better nutrition and improved health of course) but it is clear that human rights shape other values and determine a society's course.

The question the observer must ask when human rights are cast as absolutes is "how absolute and how supreme?" Are liberty and freedom absolutes and if so why the differences between those who proclaim that a particular nation must become to the world "the party of liberty" and others who insist the nation's political tradition is one of "liberty conceived in relation to equality?" If liberty is the universal value for one group of nations, is it also universal for all nations including those struggling to establish some semblance of political order? How can liberty or order or security be absolutes if one and then another is more absolute or supreme than the others at different stages in that society's development? And if different societies embrace different values what are we to make of the moral absolutes each embrace?

The founding fathers, according to the late Professor Edward S. Corwin, were uneasy about political absolutes within the political and constitutional process. The first ten amendments to the American Constitution were determinative not in and of themselves but because they reflected "the higher law." The values which were absolutes for the founders rested on certain higher principles concerning man and nature and nature's God. The human rights of the first ten amendments were in reality shadows on Plato's cave, not the causes of the shadows. They reflected truths about the nature of man, that man was both good and evil, requiring both freedom and restraints or checks and balances. Jeffersonians and Federalists might come and go proclaiming the supremacy of one right or another but "the higher law" endured. The task was to translate and interpret "the higher law" within the constitutional and political framework.

Once men began to doubt the possibility of a "higher law" and objective moral principles outside the political process they began to invest proximate political principles with all the sanctity of "the higher law." If objective principles of justice are ruled out, then a particular version of justice becomes an absolute. When the question is asked justice for whom, a group, a nation or a social class comes forward and their concept of justice takes the place of the more general principle. Reinhold Niebuhr who passed through his own stages of intellectual growth from liberalism to Marxism to democratic socialism to Christian realism was able to hold up a standard at every stage against which to measure contemporary expressions of social and political justice. In his political and moral philosophy, justice was not immanent within the political system but was a reflection of love (and its only politically attainable form). Moreover, justice in political practice represented an attempt to realize a higher justice expressed by John Dewey in the principle of "giving each man his due." In the process, power and virtue, coercion and moral principle become intermingled as societies move closer to some practical realization of justice for all. Niebuhr's absolutes weren't refuted by history as were those of some contemporary statesmen and political systems because his absolutes transcended history—and in another sense so did those of the founding fathers.

Whenever history seems to refute political absolutes that are held too closely within the political system, a second approach to human rights appears to take over. Then political strategists replace political theologians; cynicism supersedes moralism. I will not dwell too long on the rivalry between nations that have their own slightly tarnished and differing views of human rights. I would rather stress the place of human rights within the domestic political arena. Domestic political pressures, often sparked by foreign policy controversies, lead to the expansion and contraction of definitions of human rights in particular countries. As external conflicts intensify, states justify themselves not only to the world but to their own people by acting against an enemy, whether real or imagined, within. I must acknowledge American failings and lapses during the era of McCarthyism but with equal candour I cannot forebear pointing to recent treatment of dissidents within the Soviet Union. Nor are the constraints wholly political. They are both political and economic. The United States in an era of retrenchment is likely to do less for the underprivileged; moreover, the rest of the world has been saddened by the shrinkage of economic rights in the Soviet Union due to housing and medicine shortages, agricultural failures and social problems. Perhaps our rivalries would be less severe if we were more forthright about the darker side of our own histories and our common predicaments and if we were less self-righteous about achievements.

For the western countries, domestic politics poses a serious dilemma for human rights. Periodically, human rights are good politics in democracies but leaders who seize on human rights as a political issue become politically vulnerable. Totalitarian and authoritarian regimes may be successful in controlling broad swings of the political pendulum, although less so than they once claimed as 1956, 1968, and recent events in Poland attest. Western democratic leaders are endlessly tempted to overstate their mandate, with the notable exception of a political genius like Franklin D. Roosevelt, and invite an opposite political cycle. Until recently, political strategists reassured their political candidate and political party that overselling a foreign policy was politically less perilous than overselling a domestic program. (The chickens are more likely to come home to roost on economic and social promises closer to home.) However detente and human rights are but the most recent examples which throw such political strategy into question. President Carter was challenged and turned back by the electorate not because Americans had lost faith in basic human rights and fundamental freedoms; the fate of Ernest LeFever proves quite the opposite. Rather Carter's human rights policies were questioned because some of his aides promised too much and in their zeal seemed on the point of running roughshod over those responsible for other dimensions of American foreign policy, especially SALT. There is a significant difference between human rights controlling foreign policy and human rights as a vital aspect of foreign policy.

Furthermore, writers such as Elizabeth Drew in analyzing the Carter human rights policy questioned whether the Carter administration, while demonstrating naivety and moral absolutism, was also using human rights to rebuild a domestic political coalition of labor, liberals, churchmen, southern conservatives and Jews. They noted that human rights as a domestic political issue fit Carter like a glove. It became *the* issue with the most political assets and fewest liabilities. But foreign policy, whether judged as primary or not, has its own imperatives. As Lincoln, whatever his personal and private views of slavery, was guided by the need to preserve the Union, President Carter's human rights policy in its application was influenced by the dictates of national interest.

It is too early to forecast the fate of the new administration. Few informed writers doubt that candidate Reagan in 1980, as candidate Carter in 1976, approached human rights in a political context. If anything, the new administration runs the risk of making an even narrower and more complex political objective a moral absolute. Terrorism has too many morally ambiguous dimensions and is too deeply rooted in the changing international order to guarantee political success for those who promise its early demise. In the election of 1980, the elimination of terrorism did have strong appeal for those who are deeply offended by domestic and international disorder. Yet if the Carter administration failed in its first six months to shape a policy on human rights to go along with a political and moral strategy, the report card for the Reagan administration on terrorism was hardly more impressive.

I have been outspoken on this subject. I would warn colleagues from other countries that I find no lack of political cynicism in their approach to human rights. If the subject were not the fate of individual human beings everywhere, discourse might be more indirect and obscure. For every country, I see self-righteousness or moral absolutism as an enemy of human rights, but equally political cynicism is an enemy using human rights as an instrument of domestic politics. To pit differing versions of human rights or their denial, against versions put forward by one's political rival as a means of gaining political power or preserving it, may constitute a grave threat to human rights.

The third approach to human rights is moral reasoning. It has an ancient if forgotten history. In a nutshell, it requires balancing what is morally desirable with what is politically possible. Moral reasoning assumes that political choice goes on among competing goods, not between absolute right and wrong. Domestically, freedom is a noble moral purpose but it must compete with order and security. Economic growth is essential but its attainment is not justified at the price of environmental degradation. We are embarrassed to talk about the relationship of certain national goals. President Lyndon B. Johnson told Americans they need not choose between guns and butter and I have often been surprised that political scientists from the east leave unmentioned the competition between rising military expenditures and the social and economic rights they applaud.

By contrast, we are all aware as individuals of the conflicts of choice we face in personal life. All of us seek scholarly participation and advancement but most of use feel equally an obligation to our families. Modern society multiplies rather than reduces such conflicts, however much we speak of returning to a simpler life. Distances pull us apart. Megalopolis breeds social remoteness. Most of us live out our little lives with more secondary than primary contacts. The mass media in every country with all its promise of abundant public education and information leaves us puzzled and perplexed about our world. Technology exceeds comprehension. A top political advisor to President Johnson, as we have seen, confessed nuclear science was beyond him and his only choice was to pick as a guide an informed scientist he could trust, presumably politically as well as scientifically.

The concept of moral reasoning as the basis for a human rights approach would have nations and their leaders straightforwardly assess the prospects and limitations of human rights initiatives. It would ask that whenever possible policy analysis precede political declarations. It would urge nations to practice the art of placing themselves in others' shoes. History is replete with cultural and political ignorance—the Americans in Vietnam, the Russians in Afghanistan. The story is told—and I would invite Russian colleagues to match it—of South Vietnamese peasants relocated and brought together in rural hamlets. Those who planned their transfer, which brought them security from Vietcong incursions and was successful as far as it went, unfortunately forgot the importance of Vietnamese of continuing to live near their ancestral burial grounds.

Finally, moral and political choice, notwithstanding the utopians of the right and left, has its tragic elements. In every policy choice, a particular good is sacrificed in the interest of another good. What is true in personal life and taken in stride, is even more self-evident in national and international politics. Self-development and independence for children has its pattern for devoted and self-sacrificial parents. Liberalism and Marxism alike seek to root out tragedy from the human drama but profoundly misunderstand the human condition thereby. All human wisdom is not contained in our political creeds and the sooner we accept this, the better we will appreciate their strengths.

## B. Moral Reasoning in the International Arena

A major difficulty we face in advancing human rights worldwide stems from our ignorance of the international arean. Either we equate the world with a given political culture seeking to remake it in our image (if civil rights in the south in America why not the world or if low cost housing or free education in the USSR why not everywhere?) or we assume nations are without constraints in enforcing human rights wherever they choose.

I would urge the representatives and human rights spokesman of every nation to prepare a history of the landmarks in their nation's historical efforts to intervene around the world in defense of their most cherished moral and political principles. What has been a nation's history in defending their version of human rights abroad? I have no idea of the detailed picture one would find. Of one thing, however, I am sure. Whatever the merits of a nation's cause, I am confident that when it sought to act abroad, it would be faced by material and geopolitical limits.

The lesson in this regard for Americans came early in our history. President Washington was admonished by a noisy body of the citizenry mobilized by a Frenchman, Citizen Genet, to intervene on the side of revolutionary France in its struggles with successive coalitions. Although the president was burned in effigy, he resisted those who urged him to engage limited American power in an ideological crusade far from our shores and history proved him right.

The debate over the Monroe Doctrine is a second landmark. In 1820 as the debate began, both John Quicny Adams, who later changed his position, and James Monroe favored a joint declaration with Britain against further colonization in the Western Hemisphere. (Adams was also concerned to resist Russia's extending its offshore rights for fishing and trading as far south as the fifty-first parallel.) By 1823, the main issue became one between Monroe supported by Jefferson and Madison who favored support for nationalist movements such as Greek independence and revolution in Spain and Adams who insisted the United States could not effectively and with consistency oppose new European attempts at colonization in South America or on its Pacific Coast while intervening itself on the European continent. The debate raged on in the halls of congress. Edward Everett and other editors denounced Adams for abandoning America's mission and the moral purposes it shared with Europe. Others asked, going beyond Adams, how, with a frigate and a schooner, the United States could effectively support freedom off the shores of Greece. In the end, Adams and his friends prevailed. The process by which they arrived at their conclusion was moral and political reasoning. (I know of no national debate in which legislators laid out the reasons for their position more clearly and honestly unless it was the debate in the House of Commons when Prime Minister Winston S. Churchill returned from the Yalta Conference.)

Another test came in the Polk administration when America as well as France and Britain were invited by an insurgent group to take power in northern Mexico. The United States affirmed for itself and the Europeans the Monroe Doctrine. In the Civil War, at a moment of American weakness, the French sought to install a puppet ruler in Mexico only to confront the enduring precepts of the Monroe Doctrine. Throughout the nineteenth century, every time American leaders, most often out of power, sought to rally the public to intervene in the name of freedom on the European continent, they were defeated.

The twentieth century ushered in a change, but even then Woodrow Wilson's attempt to make worldwide the idea of national self-determination or, as he put it, to universalize the Monroe Doctrine, met effective opposition and he was defeated by the Senate. Franklin D. Roosevelt needed immense political skill to lead the American people to support the Grand Alliance against Hitler's tyranny. The universality of the Truman Doctrine would have been far more limited in practice than in theory but for Korea. John Foster Dulles' liberation policy turned out to be more a domestic political slogan than a viable basis for foreign policy.

Thus, even in the twentieth century, the United States has had to weigh its human rights principles against the realities of power. It has proved far easier to make resounding declarations than to support them with effective foreign policies and I very much suspect the same could be said reviewing the political history of other countries in whatever form the debate has been joined. One thinks of this when one stands on the Midway of the University of Chicago in the midst of memorials to Polish and Eastern European independent leaders of the mid-nineteenth century for whose right to national self-determination Americans spoke out but whom America did not defend.

## C. Some More Modest Proposals

In the face of all these limitations, imposed by the nature of the international system, are there more modest initiatives in defense of human rights that may be proposed? I believe there are. Some are inherent in the work of particular international bodies, for example, the International Red Cross. All nations share or ought to share a common interest in certain specific human and humanitarian rights whether in war or peace. Other target areas suggest themselves and some progress has been made in their support, for example, opposition to political torture and scrutiny of political detention. Not only target areas but to officials of the Carter administration target countries provide a focus. A few of us made this proposal without response at a conference in June of 1977. It might be better if other nations championing human rights fuelling greater violence, unless violence rather than resolution of human rights in sovereignties where they had leverage than continuously judging one another in abstract moral terms. The United Nations itself might be used as an effective means for modest advancement rather than a battleground for ideological warfare on certain human rights barely approximated by the protagonists. Within nations, intellectual and political leaders can more usefully look at specific human rights cases on factual and empirical grounds rather than encourage internecine ideological combat.

The human problem in every country is demanding enough to justify a practical agenda rather than an ideological scorecard. The human rights debate too often has been presented as a closed chapter as if preempted by a few powerful countries. We need more knowledge about the content of human rights for the majority of mankind. The most weighty question about the future of human rights, a third world philosopher has written, is the development by the great powers of the necessary tension between their sense of righteousness and an awareness of the limits of their own moral base. They will be judged, and their views of human rights judged, not alone by declarations but by human contacts along a broad front with other peoples around the world. Not only heads of state but other spokesmen can articulate views of human rights. It may even be that some human rights are better served if they remain unarticulated and if national communities and the international community busy themselves in creating favorable circumstances for human rights rather than preaching to and hectoring one another. A quiet and indirect attack may be more helpful than divisive public rhetoric. Sometimes political leadership requires anticipating problems and acting so they remain manageable without fuelling greater violence, unless violence rather than resolution or problems is the objective.

Our position as friends of human rights would be more hopeful if we openly acknowledged we are just beginning to understand effectiveness in advancing human rights. We had better be cautious in claiming that one method and one only promised progress: monitoring, declarations, covenants or penalties for violations. In no other area is it so tempting to structure programs and proclaim policies designed to make people feel good about their own efforts as individuals and nations without advancing the cause of human rights in the slightest. The British historian, Michael Howard, has written that: "Political activity takes place in a two-dimensional field—a field which can be defined by the two coordinates of ethics and power." The ethical or vertical coordinate represents the purposes of society; the horizontal coordinate capacity or ability to effect the environment. The course of ethical action is the point at which ethics and power meet. The statesman or leader pursuing his diagonal course must be like a pilot reading his compass bearing from which he cannot diverge too far in either direction. Too fantical a concern with moral absolutes may destroy the capacity for effective action; too little concern for ethical values may destroy a people's moral standing and national prestige. In Reinhold Niebuhr's words: "Politics will, to the end of history, be an area where conscience and power meet, where the ethical and coercive factors of human life will interpenetrate and work out their tentative and uneasy compromises." No one has stated so poignantly the issues that arise and confound mankind in the late twentieth century.

# IV. AMERICAN VALUES AND AMERICAN FOREIGN POLICY

## CHAPTER NINE
## INTERESTS, VALUES, AND THE AMERICAN
## CONSENSUS ON FOREIGN POLICY
### David Clinton

### A. The Conflicting Demands of Statesmanship

The statesman must play to two different audiences simultaneously. His diplomacy is faced with demands from both the domestic scene (that what the state does should reflect the deeply-held values of the society) and the international environment (that the state look to its interests for its own protection and wellbeing). If a foreign policy can appeal to both audiences it will be accounted successful, and it is likely to rally a consensus of public support that will sustain it in times of uncertainty and danger. Consensus is unlikely to be achieved or to last if a nation's policies are unbalanced. If they do not appeal to a sense of values, the public may reject them in revulsion; if they neglect national interests, they may be discarded after they lead to catastrophe.

When a concern for values and a regard for interests are mixed in the proper proportions, each leavens the other and successful diplomacy is made easier. But the task of blending the one with the other is a difficult one, the more so because no set recipe exists. Judgment, steadiness, the capacity to learn from history, and even a willingness to engage in some trial and error are all useful to the foreign policy chef, and, in the long run, the proof of the policy must be in the consensus it evokes.

"In the long run" because even a defective policy may gain popular support for a time, before its flaws (whether they be related to the country's values or to its interests) appear. Such a policy may appeal to values characterized by the shallowest moralism or to interests of the narrowest and most immediate kind, but its deficiencies will eventually be revealed and the policy itself will stand exposed as hollow. The American policy of neutrality in 1939-41, for example, was broadly consonant with the traditional

American value of remaining aloof from foreign wars, and, so far as can be determined, it reflected the sentiments of most of the country. But because it took too little heed of the international situation with which it was meant to deal, to the dangers that situation posed, and to the interests it threatened, it was shattered by the Japanese attack on Pearl Harbor and abandoned immediately thereafter. Likewise, no matter how tirelessly the turn-of-the-century advocates of imperial expansion attempted to demonstrate that their course served the nation's interests, they could not overcome the popular conviction that colonial possessions were repugnant to American values, and other policies followed. Neither neutrality nor colonialism was capable of responding both to the values Americans professed at home and to the interests the country asserted abroad, and both were superceded.

It will not do, it must be said, to draw any distinction too sharply between a domestic polity so well ordered and selfless it cares only for values, and an international state of nature so anarchic and threatening that it forces the policy-maker to deal only in interests. Any abstraction of a phenomenon as richly varied as international politics necessarily gives added prominence to some aspects of reality and slights others, and therefore should not be taken as representing the whole. The relations of the United States with other countries are guided not only by interests but also by ideals and values, both those of individual nations and those of the "world community," however fragile and tendentious it sometimes appears. Alexander Hamilton, no soft-minded idealist, recognized the place of values in international politics when he said.

> . . .[In] national controversies, it is of real importance to conciliate the good opinion of mankind. . . . Though nations, in the main, are governed by what they suppose their interest, he must be imperfectly versed in human nature who thinks it indifferent whether the maxims of a State tend to excite kind or unkind dispositions in others, or who does not know that these dispositions may insensibly mould or bias the views of self-interest.[1]

And the domestic scene is not unaquainted with interest as a standard for judging foreign policy. Economic, ethnic, and ideological interest groups seek to shape American policy abroad in ways most favorable to their particular interests. But beyond that, the public has a sense of an overall national interest. "This does not mean," as Henry Fairlie has said, "that they understand. . .every detail of any problem of foreign policy. But they do know that there is such a thing as the national interest; they have their own sense of it; and they rightly identify their own interests and even their lives with it.[2]

Nevertheless, the generalization remains true that the statesmen may often be guided by values at home where he would be forced to confine himself to interests abroad. When the protection of a set of procedural safeguards, general agreement on the ends of political action, and an effective agency of enforcement are present, as they are in domestic politics, there is more latitude for a sometimes self-denying attachment to ideals. When the statesman is faced with the rigors of a conflictual and often violent self-help system, as he is in much of international politics, his responsibility to the state and the society he represents drives him to greater reliance on self-interest. The challenge of foreign policy is that to be lastingly successful it must remain in tune with the values of the society from which it springs, while not losing touch with the diplomatic realities with which it must contend.

Moreover, success also requires that a sense of this tension and of the means by which the statesman proposes to resolve it be conveyed to the public. For the United States at any rate, the days of Cabinet diplomacy are past, and, for better or worse, foreign policy cannot remain hidden from popular scrutiny. Officials must communicate to the public the substance of their policy and the reasoning behind it in order to seek support. They may do this by their actions, of course, but they may also do it by their public statements. Major speeches and addresses, whether written or oral, are the means by which statesmen seek to mold the atmosphere in which their actions are perceived and judged, and therefore it will not do to dismiss them as "mere words." President Carter was surely correct when he spoke of his belief "that it is a mistake to undervalue the power of words and of the ideas that words embody." "In the life of the human spirit, words *are* actions," the president said,[3] and they do create a framework of thought which allows us to interpret actions and give some order to them. Even when they are insincere or self-serving, they provide clues as to what officials think will be popular with the public and will therefore help to establish or strengthen a popular consensus in favor of a foreign policy doctrine. Thus, this essay, while it will also refer to actions taken by American decision-makers from 1969 to 1981, will give a major part of its attention to their words—to significant public statements, prepared in advance, presumably in the hope of educating or persuading public opinion. It will begin, however, with an examination of what preceded that period.

## B. The Collapse of the Containment Consensus

It was its success in meeting all the criteria for popular backing that explained the durability of the American consensus in support of containing Russian/Communist expansion. From roughly 1948 to 1968 American political leaders, and behind them the American public at large, stood united in their acceptance of containment as the guiding principle of U.S. foreign policy. The doctrine was rejected on the right and the left only at the furthest ends of the political spectrum; disputes among the majority at the center, while numerous and often rancorous, were nonetheless over the interpretation and application of containment in specific cases, not over the validity of the doctrine itself. Such a consensus was due to the consonance of containment with both values and interests.

Containment rested on American values. Anti-communism, for all its excesses, particularly in the United States itself in the 1950s, grew out of the country's attachment to liberal values and to the repugnance Americans spontaneously experienced as they watched those freedoms which their political culture regarded as "unalienable rights" routinely crushed in the Soviet Union and in all other countries that internal upheavals or foreign conquest placed under communist rule. Religious persecution in those nations added a special urgency to resist the system that practiced it. Confronting such tyranny, containment could plausibly be described as a defense of personal liberty. Moreover, because of the tight control exercised by Moscow over communist parties almost everywhere, the spread of its influence seemed to threaten the freedom not only of individuals but of states and peoples as well. Thus, efforts to further containment were also efforts in support of national self-determination, another long-standing American value. This was the sense in which the much-maligned phrase, "the Free World," was accurate—not that all the countries encompassed within it had liberal democratic forms of government, but that they all had the freedom to take decisions on both internal and external policies without the fear of intervention by "socialist internationalism" if they displayed too much independence. And anticolonialism could, without too much difficulty, be fitted into containment by persuading the West European imperial powers that satisfying the natural desire of colonial peoples for emancipation was the only way to prevent them from turning to the greater tyranny of Marxism-Leninism.

Containment also served American national interests. It was of course intended to stop Soviet expansion with its attendant accretions of power that might be used to threaten the United States. To that end, it attempted to shore up the position of allies and maintain an international distribution of power favorable to its alliance structure. And in this sense revisionists are correct in saying that the Free World was a self-interested construction, an effort to preserve as wide a field as possible for Western economic and security arrangements. Containment was as much a tool of the national interest as any balance-of-power policy, of which it was only the most recent example in the history of the Westphalian state system. It was derived from interests as well as values.

But by the late 1960s, in a startlingly rapid reversal, containment, at least as it was currently being implemented, came to be seen as a threat to both American interests and American principles. Several trends in events combined to bring about this change. The Sino-Soviet split and continuing restiveness in Eastern Europe had made the image of a communist monolith centrally directed from Moscow vastly less convincing. Balance of payments difficulties, partly caused by heavy dollar expenditure abroad on military bases and their personnel scattered around the world, were undermining the position of the dollar as the foundation of the international monetary system and causing strains in economic relations with the very partners the alliances had been designed to protect. Meanwhile, many of those allies remained stubbornly unreceptive to the practices of Western democracy, a state of affairs that began to prick the American conscience as it appeared that containment was being used as a justification for support of any regime, no matter how unjust, as long as it espoused anti-communism.

Beyond these factors, however, the most immediate cause of the dissolution of the containment consensus was the war in Vietnam. No matter that its principal author had said that containment was never designed for a military conflict in Asia—containment had been used by U.S. policy-makers to justify involvement in the war, and now it was made responsible for the war's ill effects. By 1969 the conflict appeared more a threat to, than a defense of, American interests. It constituted an immense commitment of physical resources, manpower, and attention to an area difficult to describe as vital to those interests. It was an irritant in relations with the country's major allies, who felt that it distracted the United States from more important tasks. In relations with the Communist world, it diverted Washington both from possible avenues of cooperation (as in the hostility toward Hanoi's supporter, Mainland China, which delayed a rapprochement with that country), and from confrontation with its rivals when necessary (as in the flaccid response to Soviet invasion of Czechoslovakia in 1968). The war also outraged many Americans' sense of values. The casualties of war and such horrors as My Lai were brought home to America every night by television, and the government in Saigon, with its undeniable instances of corruption and authoritarianism, made less than an ideal ally. Hanoi's success in portraying itself as fighting an anti-colonialist struggle only added to the current of opinion that said that containment was betraying the values it had been adopted to protect. Deprived of both the pillars that had undergirded it for twenty years, the American consensus supporting containment collapsed.

## C. Interests Triumphant:
## The Nixon-Ford-Kissinger Years

Amid the ruins of containment, a new administration arrived in

Washington, having been elected at least in part because of popular frustration with the way in which foreign policy in general and the Vietnam War in particular were being conducted. Its response to the new environment, both at home and abroad, was significant. The newly-elected president, Richard Nixon, accepted much of the analysis of the moderate critics of containment, but then proposed his own solutions. Thus, he accepted the charge that U.S. commitments abroad had become overextended, but not the neo-isolationist response that some saw in the plea of Senator George McGovern to "come home, America." He accepted the necessity of reducing Cold War tensions, but not their suggested replacement by an idealistic effort to build a New International Economic Order.

Instead, Nixon, followed by his successor as president, Gerald Ford, and guided by his national security adviser and later secretary of state, Henry Kissinger, formulated a new basis for American foreign policy, based on interests. That the concept of interest was to be the touchstone for American policy could be clearly seen in the first of the yearly "State of the World" messages initiated by the new administration, delivered on February 18, 1970. Dean Rusk, a staunch adherent of containment, had been quoted as saying, "Other nations have interests, but the United States has responsibilities." Nixon turned the formulation on its head:

> It is misleading. . .to pose the fundamental question so largely in terms of commitments. Our objective, in the first instance, is to support our *interests* over the long run with a sound foreign policy. The more that policy is based on a realistic assessment of our and others' interests, the more effective our role in the world can be. We are not involved in the world because we have commitments; we have commitments because we are involved. Our interests must shape our commitments, rather than the other way around.'

This basing of U.S. policy on interests manifested itself in several ways. First, there was the immediately pressing problem of the war and the larger difficulty of a general sense that American commitments had been over-extended. The response of the new administration was to treat this as a matter of redefining the U.S. national interest in the Third World.

Over the course of a generation the definition of national interest used to implement and direct containment had been expanded from its traditional sense of protecting the nation's territory and independence, the lives of its people, and the military and economic security of its institutions. The emergence of a bipolar world and its division along ideological as well as power-political lines had made each superpower acutely sensitive to shifts anywhere in the world that might rebound to the benefit of its rival. If large parts of the former colonial areas of the world fell under communist rule and adopted closed political systems, the loss to the United States could be more than one of prestige, so the argument ran. Stripped of its sense that its ideals represented the wave of the future and surrounded by states espousing a hostile ideology, the U.S. itself might feel forced to adopt a siege mentality and abandon its democratic way of life. It was, in the words of Walt W. Rostow, a national security adviser to Presidents Kennedy and Johnson, therefore the American national interest that the societies of Eurasia develop along the lines broadly consistent with the nation's ideology."[5] This concern with maintaining a congenial global environment for American values led to a succession of American attempts to influence the course of Third World nations—from the Truman Doctrine to the "pactomania" of John Foster Dulles in the Eisenhower administration to the concern of the Kennedy administration with "wars of national liberation" and counterinsurgency to the debacle of Vietnam.

The Nixon administration accepted the conventional critique of this view in its main points: that the Soviet Union's own difficulties made it a less attractive model for newly-independent nations; that nationalist sentiment made these countries more resistant to long-term Soviet control through invasion or subversion than had previously been thought; that, whatever their ideological coloration, Third World nations would be guided by their interests and thus would not, for example, arbitrarily break off economic relations with the U.S.; and that, due to this reason and to the fact that there was no longer a monolithic communist international, the nature of the regimes in these countries made less difference to the global balance of power than had previously been believed.

The response of the president and his national security adviser was to narrow the American national interest in the underdeveloped world, to assert that that interest was less vital than prior administrations had claimed it to be, and to devote fewer resources to it. "[T]he United States will participate in the defense and development of allies and friends," the president proclaimed, but "America cannot—and will not—conceive *all* the plans, design *all* the programs, execute *all* the decisions and undertake *all* the defense of the free nations of the world. We will help where it makes a real difference and is considered in our interest."[6]

To put into practice this policy of narrowed national interest and reduced effort, both in Vietnam to end American involvement in the war and elsewhere to prevent similar involvements in the future, the Administration issued the Nixon Doctrine. As outlined in the President's "silent majority" speech of November 3, 1969, the new Doctrine had three points:

— First, the United States will keep all of its treaty commitments.

— Second, we shall provide a shield if a nuclear power threatens the freedom of a nation allied with us or of a nation whose survival we consider vital to our security.
— Third, in cases involving other types of aggression, we shall furnish economic and military assistance when requested in accordance with our treaty commitments. But we shall look to the nation directly threatened to assume the primary responsibility for providing the manpower for its defense.[7]

The United States would thus back up interests now considered marginal with a lessened commitment of resources. If there was fighting to be done, in most cases indigenous forces rather than American troops would do it. And while economic and military aid would rise, at least over the short run, in order to allow these nations to take over more of the responsibility for their own defense, these costs would be more than outweighed by the savings effected by closing local U.S. bases, and net American expenditures would decline.

And if present commitments were to be honored only at lower levels of effort, new ones would be entered into only reluctantly. "We will view new commitments in the light of a careful assessment of our own national interests and those of other countries, of the specific threats of those interests, and of our capacity to counter those threats at an acceptable risk and cost," the president said, with the clear implication that such a three-fold test would be very difficult to meet.

If in relations with Third World nations the thrust of Nixon policies was to downplay previously-asserted interests, in superpower relations it was to discover new ones. During his academic career, Kissinger had been an acid critic of many efforts by prior administrations to improve relations with the Soviet Union, calling them exercises in atmospherics, unrelated to the difficult problems separating the two countries, and thus inherently unstable and short-lived. A thaw in the Cold War, to be lasting, had to persuade both powers that their interests were engaged in a reduction of tensions. Efforts at relaxation from 1969 on, therefore, were aimed at the discovery of common interests:

All nations—and we are no exception—have important national interests to protect. But the most fundamental interest of all nations lies in building the structure of peace. In partnership with our allies, secure in our own strength, we will seek those areas in which we can agree among ourselves and with others to accommodate conflicts and overcome rivalries. We are working toward the day when *all* nations will have a stake in peace, and will therefore be partners in its maintenance.[8]

Detente was in essence an effort to engage the Soviet Union in enough cooperative endeavors, and hold out the prospect of enough more, to convince it that respecting American interests and accommodating itself to bargains with the West would be more profitable than self-assertion for immediate advantage, which would put at risk the common interests. A more cautious and prudent, less aggressive and menacing, attitude in Moscow was the anticipated result:

> We do not, of course, expect the Soviet Union to give up its pursuit of its own interests. We do not expect to give up pursuing our own. We do expect, and are prepared to demonstrate, self-restraint in the pursuit of those interests. We do expect a recognition of the fact that the general improvement in our relationship transcends in importance the kind of narrow advantages which can be sought only by imperilling the cooperation between our two countries.[9]

Calculations of advantage, rather than professions of goodwill, were to be the mechanism relied upon.

This confidence in interests as the key to an easing of the Cold War was symptomatic of a more general belief in the overall deideologization of international politics. With the passage of time and the loosening of ties binding together the camps of both East and West, ideology was coming to be seen as a less and less effective way of viewing the world and determining one's policies. National interests, not the political coloration of governments, acted as the most powerful influence on national actions, and American doctrine, after the rhetorical excesses of the past quarter century, would respond accordingly:

> It will be the policy of the United States. . .not to employ negotiations as a forum for cold-war invective, or ideological debate. We will regard our Communist adversaries first and foremost as nations pursuing their own interests as *they* perceive these interests, just as we follow our own interests as we see them. We will judge them by their actions as we expect to be judged by our own. Specific agreements, and the structure of peace they help build, will come from a realistic accommodation of conflicting interests.[10]

This was the touchstone asserted by the administration, not only for relations with the U.S.S.R., but also for those with the People's Republic of China and the countries of Eastern Europe.

While the Western allies for the most part applauded America's moves toward detente with the Soviet Union, her opening to China, and her willingness to negotiate agreements with East European nations, such as the treaty on the status of Berlin concluded in 1974, they were less enthusiastic about the effect of deideologization on their own relations with Washington. If bipolarity and ideological competition had tended to make the United States more suspicious of those in the rival camp than an observer looking solely at interests would have thought necessary, so too they had drawn the U.S. closer to its allies than interests alone might have dictated. Political and cultural similarities and philosophical affinities had provided a bias in American foreign policy in favor of Western Europe, Japan, and other countries around the world that could claim to be present or potential fellow democracies. Now that bias was gone. "We assumed [in the past], perhaps too uncritically, that our basic interests would be assured by our long history of cooperation, by our common cultures and our political similarities," the president said in 1973, indicating that that assumption no longer existed."

A world in which power was more evenly distributed and relations were conducted on the basis of interests rather than stable ideological alignments began to look increasingly like a return to something like the classical balance of power. This perception in both East and West was only strengthened by Nixon's statement in an interview in 1972 that "I think it will be a safer world and a better world if we have a strong, healthy United States, Europe, Soviet Union, China, Japan, each balancing the other, not playing one against the other, an even balance." " In a full-fledged balance-of-power system, each of the five actors would be as likely and congenial a partner of the United States as any other. Deideologization removed an a priori link among the U.S., Japan, and Western Europe, and replaced it with an issue-by-issue assessment of interests.

Loosened ties with the Western alliance partners were also a consequence of the fourth facet of the 1969-77 attempt to conduct foreign policy on the basis of interests—the greater concentration in Washington on *self*-interest. If the major emphasis was to be on finding and building on areas of agreement with Moscow, and if a diffusion of power among several centers, "each balancing the other," was the wave of the future, then alliance solidarity became less important. The allies could expect the U.S. to be less assiduous in consulting them and less willing to accommodate their interests in its decisions. A world grown accustomed to an America concerned with alliance interests would see it redirect its attention to national interests.

The progression in American public statements on this score was fairly clear. In 1971, the president's message on foreign policy observed that national interests among the allies would differ: "Obviously, the Western countries do not have identical national concerns and cannot be expected to agree automatically on priorities or solutions. Each ally is the best judge of its own national interest." By 1972, the language was a bit more blunt; the United States would not only recognize that it had its own national interests, but would be more vigorous in pressing them: "The future health of our friendship is not served by ignoring our differences. Nor is it served by expectations that [a member of the alliance] will subordinate its interests in order to maintain an atmosphere of perfect amity." A year later, the message was stiffer still. Washington would not back down from its interests merely to avoid a public row with its allies; nor would it be satisfied with ritualistic protestations that sought to paper over the issue at hand: "Mature countries do not expect to avoid disputes or conflicts of interests. A mature alliance relationship, however, means facing up to them on the basis of mutuality. It means seriously addressing the underlying causes, not the superficial public events." [13]

In accordance with these sentiments, the administration reduced the sacrifices it was willing to make for the sake of Western unity. It reduced its troop commitments in many locations overseas under the Nixon Doctrine, and although it opposed congressional efforts to remove troops from Europe, it did demand that the NATO partners pay a larger share of the costs involved. Japan was presented with the two "Nixon shocks" in 1971—that of the announcement of the president's trip to China on July 15 and that of his stern New Economic Policy on August 15. All American trading partners had to accept the latter's unilateral suspension of the convertibility of the dollar into gold and imposition of a ten percent import surcharge. "There is no longer any need," the president asserted in his speech to the nation presenting his economic program, "for the United States to compete with one hand tied behind her back," [14] and in the negotiations to shore up the international monetary system that followed, America's competitors were more than once reminded of this by the tough talk of Treasury Secretary Connally.

In short, the administration's analysis of foreign policy—with allies, adversaries, and nonaligned nations; in political, military, and economic affairs—was suffused with talk of interests. Values, by contrast, were de-emphasized. Idealistic rhetoric led to unrealistic expectations, lent itself to the ungrounded atmospherics that Kissinger distrusted, and could introduce unnecessary rigidities into international affairs. Better to let the American penchant for moralizing lie.

This relative neglect was made easier by the administration's limited conception of the role public opinion should play in foreign policy. Acquiescence more than enthusiasm was desired, for an untutored public did not have the skills to deal effectively with the more complex world that both the Administration and its critics agreed was emerging. Too much public interest in foreign policy could be channelled into moral crusades, or satisfying but ultimately ineffective actions like the Jackson-Vanik Amendment. Public opinion could grow attached to some countries, cold toward others, thus impairing the flexibility that shifting interests required. Public outcry for "taking a stand" could undermine the efforts of "quiet diplomacy." Public inexpertness made it difficult to convey the interests at stake and the subtle maneuvers frequently needed to protect them. Centralized policy-making focused on the President, the National Security Adviser, and the staff of the National Security Council promised better results.

## D. The Attack on Nixon-Ford-Kissinger Policies

This conception of foreign policy came under scathing attack in the 1976 campaign. The Democratic nominee, Jimmy Carter, had made it clear that he rejected both any distinction between foreign and domestic policy and the administration's reliance on interest as the country's guide in international affairs: "A nation's domestic and foreign policies [sic] actions should be derived from the same standards of ethics, honesty and morality which are characteristic of the individual citizens of the nation. The people of this country are inherently unselfish, open, honest, decent, competent, and compassionate. Our government should be the same, in all its actions and attitudes." [15] This was so, at least partly because the nation's strength ultimately derived from its principles:

> We have an inevitable role of leadership to play. . . . But our foreign policy ought not be based on military might nor political power nor economic pressure.
> It ought to be based on the fact that we are right and decent and honest and truthful and predictable and respectful; in other words, that our foreign itself accurately represents the character and the ideals of the American people.

Tapping this power required the abandonment of a policy that pursued equilibrium through following interests rather than principles:

> . . .the present Administration—our government—has been so obsessed with balance-of-power politics that it has often ignored basic American values and a common and proper concern for human rights. The leaders of this administration have often rationalized that there is little room for morality in foreign affairs and that we must put self-interest above principle. I disagree strongly. . .

A foreign policy centered on values would also be grounded more firmly in popular opinion:

> In looking back, almost every time we've made a serious mistake as we relate to other nations—and we've made a lot of them—it's been because the American people have basically been excluded from participation in the evolution or consum-

mation of attitudes toward other countries around the world. . . We've been excluded, we've been lied to, and we have lost the tremendous advantage of the idealism and the common sense and the basic honesty and character of the American people which should accurately exemplify and be exemplified by our nation's own character as it relates to other countries. [16]

A Democratic Convention controlled by Carter delegates adopted his attack on the amorality of the policies of the preceeding eight years, wrote into its platform an endorsement of his reaffirmation of values, and promised "a return to the politics of principle."

Carter's stance carried the day when he defeated Ford in November. This is not to say that the election turned on the Nixon-Ford-Kissinger conception of foreign policy (although Carter did give more prominence to foreign affairs than had been anticipated, given the Democratic Party's traditional advantage on domestic issues and his own inexperience in international politics). Nor does it mean that defeat of an incumbent party necessarily signifies a repudiation of the basic principles of the foreign policy it has pursued; party control of the White House changed twice during the containment years without upsetting the foreign policy consensus that governed the country.

Instead, what is striking about the debate in the election of 1976 is that the attack of Carter and the Democrats went to the heart of the Republican Administration's view of the world. Harsh charges had been traded in elections during the preceeding twenty years, but they had been primarily over means, not ends. Each party would charge that the other had adopted the wrong tactics to carry out a strategy accepted by both sides—that of containment. Ford was defeated in 1976 by those who questioned the foundation of the policy he and his predecessor had pursued—the grounding of policy in maneuvers for interests rather than aspirations for values. It was thus at least as much the nature of the attack as the fact that it succeeded which caused doubt that containment had been replaced by a new and equally-firm ground for American foreign policy. Consensus remained to be achieved, and the proponents of values now had their opportunity to do so.

## E. Values Triumphant: The Carter Years

As its predecessor had done, the values-centered policy of the Carter administration defined itself to a great extent by its rejection of what had gone before. The worldly cynicism of the former Harvard professor was to be replaced by the reforming openness of the former Georgia farmer. The virtue of continuity stressed by Ford in the campaign had been rejected by the voters in favor of the possibility of a fresh start. And the failure of a foreign policy based on interests and not values to win sustained popular support meant that it would be succeeded by one that found its roots in American values, principles, and ideals.

The new administration therefore justified its policies on various geographical and functional issues by pointing to the values they served. In his 1979 State of the Union Address, President Carter summed up the U.S. stance toward the Third World in this way: "A true world community cannot be fashioned or endure so long as the weapons of war multiply and spread, so long as ancient disputes fester and the demands of justice are unmet, so long as much of mankind remains impoverished and without hope." [17] The Carter administration agreed with the Nixon administration that the less-developed countries of the world were showing themselves to be more resistant to communist attack or subversion than American officials in the late 1950s and early 1960s had expected. But whereas Nixon took this as a signal for the United States to withdraw its own forces and extend military assistance so that these nations could defend themselves and the U.S. could devote more attention to domestic difficulties, Carter believed that it gave the U.S. an opportunity to institute reforms in the Third World without undue risk. "[W]e are now free of that inordinate fear of communism which once led us to embrace any dictator who joined us in that fear," he said in 1977 at Notre Dame. "I'm glad that's being changed." [18]

Seizing this opportunity meant following policies that rested on the three pillars of the president's 1979 statement. The first concerned the international flow of arms. While he did not move to reverse the Nixon Doctrine and have the United States reassume responsibility for the defense of much of the Third World, Carter did attempt to reduce the arms that his predecessors had thought were necessary to allow these nations to defend themselves. Saying that "Our stand for peace is suspect if we are also the principal arms merchant of the world," [19] the president imposed a declining ceiling on American arms sales abroad, and this stance on conventional weapons was complemented by a vigorous effort to persuade other countries to forego nuclear weapons by adhering to the Non-Proliferation Treaty. Freed of the necessity to pour their resources into regional arms races, the nations of the Third World could divert them to the problems represented by the second and third pillars of the administration's conception. Settlement of local and regional disputes constituted the second pillar, as exemplified in American efforts to help the parties concerned come to terms in the Middle East and Zimbabwe-Rhodesia, through the Camp David and Lancaster House agreements respectively. An end to such conflicts would itself allow more funds to be used for combatting such evils as hunger and disease, and this represented the third pillar in the United States' Third World strategy. "We know a peaceful world cannot long exist one-third rich and two-thirds hungry,"[20] the president declared, and consequently "we will fight our wars against poverty, ignorance, and injustice, for those are the enemies against which our forces can be honorably marshaled."[21] Abandonment of the weapons of war, attainment of lasting peace, improvement in the lot of populations accustomed only to suffering—these were the values President Carter's policies in the Third World were intended to serve.

If the changes in American policy toward the least powerful countries of the world sometimes seemed dramatic, those in its relations with the world's other superpower were more subtle. The broad goals of U.S. actions toward the Soviet Union from 1977 to 1981—reduced tensions and progress in arms control—were the same as those of the years between 1969 and 1977; it was in the rhetorical justification for these actions that a shift was most apparent. Detente under Nixon and Ford had been a matter solely of diplomacy, and often of diplomacy only at the highest levels; matters of "domestic politics" on either side had been excluded. Carter proposed to continue detente, but also to broaden and deepen it so that it more directly affected the two societies at large. He offered the change to Moscow in his address at the U.S. Naval Academy on June 7, 1978:

> The word 'detente' can be simplistically defined as 'the easing of tensions between nations.' The word is in practice [,] however, further defined by experience, as those nations evolve new means by which they can live with each other in peace.
>
> To be stable, to be supported by the American people, and to be a basis for widening the scope of cooperation, then [,] detente must be broadly defined and truly reciprocal. Both nations must exercise restraint in troubled areas and in troubled times. Both must honor meticulously those agreements which have already been reached to widen cooperation, naturally and mutually limit nuclear arms production, permit the free movement of people and the expression of ideas, and to protect human rights. . . .
>
> Our principal goal is to help shape a world which is more responsive to the desire of people everywhere for economic well-being, social justice, political self-determination, and basic human rights.[22]

This new definition of detente offered the Soviets both opportunities and risks. By bringing in American domestic society, it held out the prospect of establishing a solid base of support for East-West ties which could withstand the vicissitudes of political campaigns and changes of administration that had disturbed it during the 1970s. But by bringing in Soviet domestic society, through tying detente to internal social justice and human rights, it seemed to strike directly at the foundation of the communist regime's control of its own population. Both consequences flowed from the administration's desire to portray detente in the brighter shades of responsiveness to the values of the two peoples rather than the more somber tones of maintaining a stable balance of power.

This appeal to values instead of interests could also be seen in the President's attitude toward a central element of any process of reducing superpower tensions, the ongoing effort at strategic arms control. Directing his words particularly to the Soviet Union, Carter said in the Naval Academy speech, "I urge. . .that all other powers join us in emphasizing works of peace rather than weapons of war." [23] This step, too, was justified in terms of "our ultimate goal—the elimination of all nuclear weapons from this Earth," and eschewed language appropriate to a balance-of-power policy: "I would hope that the nations of the world might say that we had built a lasting peace, based not on weapons of war but on international policies which reflect our own most precious values." "This [strategic arms] race is not only dangerous, it's morally deplorable," the president told an audience at Notre Dame University in 1977. "We must put an end to it." [24] A goal at once so lofty and so distant began to take on many of the characteristics of a moral value and not a limited act of self-interest, and the bold proposals taken by Secretary of State Cyrus Vance to Moscow in the spring of 1977 seemed to have been designed with this ambitious end in mind. In the SALT talks, then, as in other facets of the United States' relationship with the Soviet Union, an appeal to values could be heard that had not been present before.

The administration asserted its intention to alter the tone of its relations with its major allies in Western Europe and Japan as well. "We are deeply convinced that the future lies not with dictatorship but democracy," Carter asserted, and "Freedom, peace, and justice are the sources of our true power on which all else must rest." This conception put the nature of a regime at the very heart of the United States' attitude toward it, and mandated a bias in favor of fellow democracies over undemocratic or otherwise unjust states—in other words, the reverse of the Kissinger policy's stated intention of dealing with the other states on the basis of the interests at stake, and not their ideology or form of government. During his campaign for the presidency, Carter had frequently criticized American foreign policy from 1969 to 1976 for its alleged tendency to make no distinction in favor of those states where freedom was most secure and, indeed, to be more solicitous of the U.S.S.R. (because of its greater power and its central place in U.S. calculations) than of the country's democratic allies. "We seek not a condominum of the powerful but a community of the free," candidate Carter promised in 1976, [26] and, once in office, he continued to reflect this concern in his public statements. "Because we are free, we can never be indifferent to the fate of freedom elsewhere," he proclaimed in his Inaugural Address. "Our moral sense dictates a clearcut preference for those societies which share with us an abiding respect for individual human rights." When he said in his 1979 State of the Union Message that "the cooperation we share with those whose purposes and traditions are closest to our own is strong and growing stronger,"[28] he was both describing American policy under his leadership and giving testimony to his belief in the importance of values in determining diplomatic alignments.

Nowhere was this stated devotion to values more evident than in the President's commitment to human rights as a touchstone of foreign policy. This determination that America would make the treatment of foreign citizens by their governments her national concern ran through the whole of Carter's four years in the White House, from his statement in his Inaugural Address that "our commitment to human rights must be absolute" to his reaffirmation in his final State of the Union Address of "a cause that is closest to my heart—human rights," and his avowal in his Farewell Address that "I believe with all my heart that America must always stand for. . .basic human rights at home and abroad."[29]

United States leadership in the struggle for human rights was appropriate, according to the president, because of the conjunction of two historical trends, one external to the country, and one internal to it. Abroad, with the process of liberating nations from colonialism largely completed, attention was turning everywhere to the need for the liberation of individuals from harsh and unjust governmental practices:

> The world itself is now dominated by a new spirit. Peoples more numerous and more politically aware are craving, and now demanding, their place in the sun—not just for the benefit of their own physical condition, but for basic human rights.
> The passion for freedom is on the rise. Tapping this new spirit, there can be no nobler nor more ambitious task for America to undertake. . .than to help shape a just and peaceful world that is truly humane.

Through fortunate historical circumstance, America stood ready to meet these demands because of its unique heritage. As a nation of immigrants, Americans were defined more than by anything else by their belief in freedom:

> America did not invent human rights. In a very real sense, it's the other way around. Human rights invented America. Ours was the first nation in the history of the world to be founded explicitly on such an idea. Our social and political progress has been based on one fundamental principle—the

value and importance of the individual. The fundamental force that unites us is not kinship or place of origin or religious preference. The love of liberty is the common blood that flows in our American veins.*³¹*

Because the United States was the right nation in the right place at the right time to advance the cause of human rights, it had an obligation to do so.

This obligation could be fulfilled in two ways. The first was the example set by the United States' respect for human rights in its domestic affairs: "Our Nation can be strong abroad only if it is strong at home. And we know that the best way to enhance freedom in other lands is to demonstrate here that our democratic system is worthy of emulation." The second was the use of the various tools of American diplomacy to persuade other countries to improve their own performance: "The effort to make human rights a central component of our foreign policy comes from our deepest sense of ourselves as a humane and freedom-loving people. We do not make our standards the precondition for every relationship we

have with other countries; yet human rights can never be far from the focus of our thinking or we violate our own best values."*³²* As part of the first effort, the president asked in 1979, and repeated the request in later years, that the Senate ratify the various pending international conventions dealing with human rights: the Convention on Racial Discrimination; the Genocide Convention; the U.N. Covenants on Political and Civil Rights, and on Economic and Social Rights; and the Inter-American Convention on Human Rights. Central to the second were the granting or withholding of U.S. assistance (especially military assistance) to other nations, and the publicity generated by, among other things, the annual reports required by Congress on the state of human rights in all countries receiving such assistance.

Through either or both of these methods, human rights became a component of American foreign policy in every area of the world. It was the issue of human rights that caused U.S. relations with some countries of the Third World to deteriorate and those with others to improve. It was the lack of human rights in the Soviet Union that complicated the U.S. drive for arms control agreements with that country, while at the same time it reminded Americans of those values which differentiated the United States from its rival, and which any agreement ought to be designed to protect. It was a common respect for human rights that led the Administration to place renewed emphasis on its ties to its major allies in Western Europe and Japan. In all these contexts, Carter said, "the purposes of our own Nation's policy" were the same: "to ensure economic justice, to advance human rights, to resolve conflicts without violence, and to proclaim in our great democracy our constant faith in the liberty and dignity of human beings everywhere."[33]

If there was one thread that bound together all these disparate elements coming under the general heading of "values in foreign policy," it was the desirability of re-establishing the links between American diplomacy and American popular feeling. Sobered by the rigidities induced by popular attachment to indiscriminate anti-communism during the period of containment, the Nixon and Ford Administrations had downplayed the need for positive public involvement in and support of American policy (as opposed to a general willingness to let decision-makers do what they thought best, without asking them too many questions). This attitude, in turn, had engendered a counter-reaction, which had helped to elect the Carter administration and guided its actions. It was the belief of the president and his subordinates that the United States could be truly strong and effective overseas only when its principles were derived from the people and not simply tolerated by them. With the American people, at any rate, the only means of drawing such a link was to appeal—explicitly and repeatedly—to American ideals. In a radio address during his campaign for re-election, Carter reminded his listeners, "I've sought to guide us in the spirit of liberty and peace. When we lose touch with that spirit, when we begin to think of our power as an end in itself, when we begin to think that the only source of respect is the threat of force, then we lose the best that is within us." The country's diplomacy also lost, so the president's thinking ran, the effectiveness with which public support endowed it, "for we know that if we despise our own Government, we have no future."[34]

This and other speeches were intended to illuminate "the strands that connect our actions overseas with our essential character as a nation." They were designed to show that "we can have a foreign policy that is democratic, that is based on fundamental values, and that uses power and influence, which we have, for humane purposes. We can also have a foreign policy that the American people both support and, for a change, know about and understand."[35]

This equilateral triangle formed by American values, popular backing, and diplomacy was to be the model for the formulation of policy:

> In our foreign policy, the separation of people from government has been in the past a source of weaknss and error. In a democratic system like ours, foreign policy decisions must be able to stand the test of public examination and public debate. If we make a mistake in this administration, it will be on the side of frankness and openness with the American people.
>
> [And, further] we are confident of the good sense of American people, and so we let them share in the process of

making foreign policy decisions. We can thus speak with the voices of 215 million, and not just of an isolated handful.[36]

It was the model for the execution and the substance of U.S. diplomacy as well:

> I promised, when I was campaigning among the American people, that when I took office,. . .I would make our foreign policy reflect our highest ideals and standards. . . .
> When I promised this country a government as good as our own people, some critics dismissed it as meaningless rhetoric. But they missed what I was really talking about. . . .
> Our foreign policy is as good as our people when we speak out for human rights around the world, and we will. Our foreign policy is as good as the American people when we work to bring peace to ancient enemies, and we have done so . . . This is true not just in this administration, but from the moment of our birth as a nation, through all times, as long as we call ourselves a free people.[37]

U.S. diplomacy was thus to be completely recast, but only to bring it back into conformity with its historical roots after the aberration of the Nixon-Ford years.

"We are a confident nation," the president asserted in a review of the accomplishments of his first year in office. "We've restored a moral base for our foreign policy."[38] The nation was confident, he implied, precisely *because* his administration had restored a moral base for its foreign policy, and had thereby regained popular support for that policy. The contrast with his predecessors was complete. The Nixon and Ford Administrations, seeing the troubles the country faced overseas, looked to American interests abroad; the Carter administration, confronted with a loss of domestic public confidence, recurred to American values at home. In its rhetoric at least, the new substitute for containment was diametrically opposed to the old.

## F. The Attack on Carter Policies

Yet, paradoxically enough, this administration which placed so much emphasis on the necessity of maintaining public enthusiasm for the guiding principles of American foreign policy found itself increasingly bereft of public confidence as it approached the end of the presidential term. As early as the spring of 1978, the president found it necessary to defend his actions abroad by denying as a "myth" the idea "that this country is somehow pulling back from protecting its interests and its friends around the world." "We shall use our great economic, technological, and diplomatic advantages to defend our interests and to promote American values," he said.[39] Led by opponents of the administration, however, public fears seemed to continue to rise that U.S. diplomacy, at least as practiced by the Carter administration, could not pursue these two goals simultaneously, and that the promotion of American values was displacing the defense of the country's interests.

Just as they had been four years before, these doubts were both crystallized and capitalized on by the opposition party and its candidates. Throughout the spring and summer, Carter's conduct of foreign policy was one of the most frequent targets of contenders in the Republican primaries (and of Senator Kennedy in the Democratic primaries), and the criticism reached a crescendo in the platform adopted by the Republican Convention in July. "For three and one-half years the Carter administration has given us a foreign policy not of constancy and credibility, but of chaos, confusion, and failure," the platform read. "It has produced an image of our country as a vacillating and reactive nation, unable to define its place in the world, the goals it seeks, or the means to pursue them"—unable, in other words, to define and defend United States national interests.

It was the charge of neglecting American interests that formed the burden of the platform's excoriation of the administration's actions overseas. This was so, for example, in the section on relations with Third World countries. Carter's restrictions on foreign arms sales had been justified in terms of his moral objections to the country's being a "merchant of death"; the Republicans criticized the ceilings in terms of the damage they did to U.S. interests:

> the manipulation of foreign arms sales has been one of the most seriously abused policy initiatives of the Carter administration. The establishment of arbitrary ceilings on foreign sales, and the complex procedural and policy guidelines governing such sales have impeded the support of U.S. foreign policy objectives abroad. . . .Republicans pledge to reform and rebuild U.S. military assistance and foreign arms sales policies so that they will serve American interests. . . .

Likewise, the document expressed doubts over the administration's public support for greatly increased U.S. foreign assistance with no immediate prospect of return: "American foreign economic assistance is not a charitable venture. . . .U.S. foreign economic assistance. . .should only be extended when it is consistent with America's foreign policy interest." The most stinging language, however, was reserved for Carter's public campaign for human rights:

> No longer should American foreign assistance programs seek to force acceptance of American governmental forms. The principal consideration should be whether or not extend-

ing assistance to a nation or group of nations will advance America's interests and objectives. The single-minded attempt to force acceptance of U.S. values and standard of democracy has undermined several friendly nations, and made possible the advance of Soviet interests in Asia, the Middle East, Africa, and in the Western Hemisphere in the past four years.

In its treatment of superpower relations, the platform also saw dangers unmet: "The scope and magnitude of the growth of Soviet military power threatens American interest at every level. . ." To deal with the problem, it promised a return to the politics of interest, although it appeared much less sanguine than the Republican administrations of the Kissinger days that the U.S. and the U.S.S.R. could soon find an overriding common interest in arms control:

> . . .unlike the Carter administration, we will not base our politics toward the Soviet Union on naive expectations, unilateral concessions, futile rhetoric, and insignificant maneuvers. . . .
> . . .Republicans will strive to resolve critical issues through peaceful negotiations, but we recognize that negotiations conducted from a position of military weakness can result only in further damage to American interests. . . .
> . . .We will pursue hard bargaining for equitable, verifiable, and enforceable agreements. We will accept no agreement for the sake of having an agreement, and will accept no agreements that do not fundamentally enhance our national security.

The party's discussion of the United States' relationship with its major allies took much the same tone. In treating matters of defense, it found a strong common interest among the Western industrialized states, though one strained by the president's moralizing: "three-and-a-half years of Carter administration policies have resulted in an increased threat to vital Alliance security interests." But on economic questions, there seemed to be a return to the more narrowly nationalistic definitions of interest sometimes espoused in the years from 1969 to 1977:

> The Republican Party believes the United States must adopt an aggressive export policy. For too long, our trade policy has been geared toward helping our foreign trading partners. Now, we have to put the United States back on the world export map. We helped pull other countries out of the post-World War II economic chaos; it is time to remedy our own crisis.

In this area of policy as in others, the American national interest was to come first.

Kissinger, when he appeared before the convention, adopted this line of attack. The country's major task, he said, was "to put an end to [the] drift, confusion, retreat and weakness" that he charged had characterized the Carter years, and instead "to restore and then uphold the political balance of power." These difficulties had been caused by a president so preoccupied with inserting moral values into every policy that he neglected the nation's interests: "The administration's reluctance to assert our interests in the early stages of a crisis—its congenital fear of our power—encourages ever growing challenges," and "these multiplying crises are the natural result of a naive philosophy which since 1977 has recoiled from our power and fled from our responsibilities."[40] His own policies, centered on a realistic sense of national interest, the former Secretary implied, would have served the country better.

Despite its doubts about the results of Kissinger's efforts at detente, the Convention agreed. Neglect of national interests was the major criticism leveled against the administration by most speakers, and the platform's demand for "a foreign policy firmly rooted in principle" was a distinctly secondary theme. "Republicans are united," the platform summarized,

> . . .in a belief that America's international humiliation and decline can be reversed only by strong presidential leadership and a consistent, farsighted foreign policy, supported by a major upgrading of our military forces, a strengthening of our commitments to our allies, and a resolve that our national interests be vigorously protected.

It was on this theme that Ronald Reagan and other Republicans waged the fall campaign, and it was this theme, among others, that helped to defeat Carter and his policies after a trial of only four years (instead of the eight that had been given the Nixon-Kissinger policies), and by a larger margin than Ford's defeat in 1976. As in 1976, defeat was at the hands, not of those who shared with the incumbent a consensus on the essentials of the nation's foreign policy and differed only on specific acts of implementation, but of those who rejected the very base of Carter's conception of what American diplomacy was all about. Thus, the second proposed replacement for containment was rejected as the first had been; the tension between interests and values had not yet been resolved.

## G. The Difficulty of Striking a Balance

For twelve years the United States has sought a foreign policy doctrine that would succeed containment as the foundation for public consensus and support, without success. Kissinger (if we may take him as the representative of the two presidents whom he served as both subordinate and mentor) emphasized the imperative of following the country's interests; Carter spoke to the need for it to return to its values; neither seemed able to substitute successfully for that blend of idealism and calculation that the American people followed during the years of the Cold War.

These failures are all the more poignant when one considers that, despite this essay's highlighting of ideas which Kissinger and Carter themselves emphasized in their public rhetoric, neither was a one-dimensional figure. Both men insisted that their policies served more than one end: Kissinger, in saying that the end of detente, "the attainment of peace[,] is a profound moral concern;" Carter, in arguing for a recognition of "those moral duties which, when assumed, seem invariably to be in our own best interests."⁴¹ Neither was wholly one-sided, as is demonstrated by Kissinger's Pacem in Terris speech and by Carter's ultimate refusal to redeem his campaign promise of cutting five to seven billion dollars from the defense budget; and the picture of Carter as a naive moralizer is as inaccurate as that of Kissinger as the victim of a moral lobotomy. Each eventually moved some distance toward the position of the other, although to their opponents it seemed rather late in the day: Kissinger's speech in Lusaka, Zambia on the necessity of responding to the forces of change in Africa came in his last year in office, 1976, and Carter's revised estimate of the intentions of the Soviet Union had to wait until that country's invasion of Afghanistan in December, 1979. By this time, each had become so firmly identified with one side or the other of the values-interests debate that his attempts to moderate his position seemed clumsy and were held up to ridicule. The derision caused by Ford's banishment of the word "detente" from the vocabulary of the White House was equalled only by that occasioned by Carter's statement that he had learned more about the Russians in the five days following their move into Afghanistan than in the preceding three years of his presidential tenure. Nevertheless, if the skeptical response to these shifts in course shows how pervasive and longlasting is the impression created by an administration's style in its first year in office, the fact that alterations were tried at all demonstrates a willingness to learn from experience that is the very opposite of a dogmatic espousal of either interests or values.

The lack of success in rallying the American people to a consensus in support of a foreign policy doctrine to replace containment suffered over twelve years by three successive presidents aided by the efforts of able, intelligent and high-minded men and women inevitably raises the question of whether success in the endeavor is possible at all. Might it not be that something like the Cold War consensus was attainable only in the unambiguous atmosphere of the postwar years? Not since its first twenty years had the country found itself facing such a sustained direct challenge to both its values and its interests. Moreover, unlike the Napoleonic Wars, which had divided Americans along ideological lines corresponding to their Anglophilic or Francophilic sentiments, the Cold War, by acting as a threat to values held by almost all Americans, united public opinion in support of government actions. If containment was in fact not a model which later policy-makers could seek to duplicate, but an aberration produced by unique historical circumstances at home and abroad, then it would seem to follow that public consensus cannot be regained under any foreseeable circumstances.[12] If an attempt is to be made to restore a reasonably hardy agreement across a broad spectrum of American popular opinion on the fundamentals of what U.S. diplomacy should seek to accomplish, however, then some attention might be given to four lines of thought outlined briefly here.

First, despite the discouraging history outlined in this essay, those concerned with making policy and with persuading the public of its merits should remain convinced of the importance of arriving at some broad conception of what United States foreign policy is all about. A guiding doctrine to which decision-makers have given some thought beforehand and in which they have tried to give both values and interests their due will likely be more balanced than decisions arrived at *ad hoc* and seriatim. Actions taken at a moment of crisis, without the prompting or restraining influence of general principles thought through beforehand, are liable to ignore any need for balance between values and interests, over-emphasizing one at the expense of the other. Short-sighted pragmatism and imprudent idealism are policy prescriptions equally inimical to the physical and political health of the nation.

So too, with the task of building and leading a body of support among the citizenry for the statesman's conception. The effort is lengthy, frustrating, laborious, and, sometimes, ultimately futile, but the alternative is worse: those who have not taken the trouble beforehand to prepare the soil of public opinion may find at a moment of crisis that in proposing a course of action in response they are casting their seed upon barren, unreceptive ground. A hasty retreat under these conditions may be a necessity, but one that leaves conditions worse than if no action at all had been taken; the statesman in a democracy may avoid such a situation only by developing and then respecting a rationale for action within the limits of which he may follow his judgment with reasonable confidence that the public will support him. In neither the international nor the domestic realm is politics static, of course; the bounds of permissible behavior may shift. Actions that were once unthinkable may become acceptable, as was demonstrated by the rapid development of Sino-American relations in the years 1969-1981. Alternatively, the confines of popular consent may narrow, as American policy-makers learned over the course of the Vietnam War. The fluid nature of public support makes the task of replenishing it difficult, never-ending, but also highly important.

Thus foreign policy doctrine helps to supply the statesman with both continuity and consensus. But what should be the nature of this doctrine? We have said that it should not solely reflect either values or interests, focussing on one to the exclusion of the other, but should instead balance both. But to say this is not to say very much. The vexing (and vital) question is not whether policy should be a blend of values and interests, but how the two should be mixed and in what proportions.

This need for further thought leads to a second proposition: that the mix of values and interests in American foreign policy need not follow the same formula in every area of the world. In his Stafford Little lectures, delivered in 1954, George Kennan discussed "the two planes of international reality"—the communist and noncommunist worlds—and the different principles U.S. diplomacy brought to each. Since then, decolonization, the loosening of ties within the blocs of both East and West, the Sino-Soviet split, and other realignments have multiplied the numbers of planes composing international politics; bipolarity is being replaced by something more intricate and subtle. Despite this new complexity, however the point remains that, especially in the means it employs, foreign policy may be more or less freighted with values, more or less constrained by interests, depending on the particular nations or groups of nations with which it is dealing. There is no reason to assume beforehand that American actions must reflect a uniform balance between values and interests everywhere, unaffected by local customs and conditions. U.S. policy toward some states may be free to be guided more by values; in other areas, it may have to be more constrained by interests. The clearest example of the discriminating judgments required may be seen in the contrast between Washington's relations with the other nations of the North Atlantic region, where the use of armed force to settle disputes seems practically inconceivable, and its dealings with the Soviet Union, where the danger of war looms as an ever-present and all-too-real threat. The end of safeguarding American security and the freedom to pursue American ideals internally remains the same in both cases, but the means differ in the extent to which they can be guided by values such as selfless sacrifice for others or submission to the rule of law. Because of a shared political tradition and a greater sense of security, the U.S. can be more "disinterested" in the former case than in the latter. The policy of containment, because it perceived a need to make sacrifices on some matters in order to achieve the more important goal of unifying the West against Soviet expansionism, and the policy of the Carter years, because it laid great stress on the respect for human freedom held in common by the U.S. and its major allies, recognized this point more clearly than the policy of the Kissinger era, which tended to speak in the undifferentiated language of interests everywhere. Any foreign policy doctrine for the years ahead, if it is to do justice to both interests and values, and thereby receive public support, must recognize that, in the effort to relate the two, this is not "one world." It is many worlds, and the balance to be struck in each of them must reflect their differences.

Third, even when the unique requirements of each geographical area have been taken into account, there remains a further source of complexity. In deciding on an action the statesman makes a choice not just between interests and values—it would be simpler if he could—but among competing values and conflicting interests as well. Reality presents a more variegated pattern than that suggested by the admittedly correct statement that values must be balanced against interests. Such a balance must indeed be struck, but values and interests may be compatible as well, and may combine in urging a particular course of action, the alternatives to which may be supported by other combinations of the two. It is rare that one option presented to a policy-maker can present itself as justified solely by ideals, while an opposing option commends itself simply by the advantages it provides. In the Indo-Pakistani war of 1971, where did justice lie—on the side of India, the democracy fighting the repressive Islamabad regime, or that of Pakistan, the nation fighting to defend its territory against the incursions of New Delhi, which was at least nominally the aggressor? In 1977, when the Carter administration announced that it would gradually remove American troops from South Korea, and in 1979, when it reversed itself, on which side of the question did American interests lie? How were they altered by the intervening two years? On both of these occasions, of course, and on others during the years discussed here, principles and interests contended on both sides of the issue. To make it clear that no one policy preference can claim a monopoly on either conscience or calculation is to take a necessary step toward the development of a foreign policy doctrine that will last. Any set of guidelines will encounter difficulties from time to time, but a mature sense of the composite nature of almost all policies can prevent temporary disappointment from turning into lasting disillusionment and a loss of consensus.

Fourth, the statesman needs to explore ways of making the national interest more compatible with the standards set by American values. This is not the same as reliance on the purity of one's intentions in the touching faith that therefore "everything will work out for the best in the end." Nor should it be equated with the prideful attitude which assumes that in following the interests of one's own country one is automatically advancing the cause of justice in the world. It is instead a more modest goal. A state may narrow its conception of the national interest by its willingness to compromise on claims whose importance is not of the first rank; a state may broaden its definition of the national interest by foregoing its own immediate and particular interests in order to futher different goals shared by other states as well. The Nixon Doctrine may stand as an example of the first course; the Carter human rights policy, of the second.

To discover that some aspects of international politics do not constitute a zero-sum game is not to sacrifice the national interest. To establish aims and devise policies that benefit other nations as well as one's own is simply to become aware of another dimension of the national interest, a dimension that might be overlooked in an over-hasty examination of immediate advantages. That some of these immediate advantages may be foregone is undeniable. But the state does so in the expectation that the compensating benefits of cooperation will be at least as great, and that prudent virtue will not go unrewarded. At the same time, assuming that the goals of other states for which one is willing to relinquish some unshared interests and concentrate on others held in common are worthy ones, the highest American values will also be advanced.

These suggestions are likely to seem fragmentary and incomplete. But if—as the record of American diplomacy since the collapse of containment appears to suggest—a consensus of public backing for United States' diplomacy can be attained only when values and interests are skillfully blended by American statesmen in its formulation, implementation, and explication, then these thoughts may illuminate the first steps to be taken on the road to re-establishing the foundations of U.S. actions abroad. The tribulations undergone by the attempts of those like Kissinger and Carter to begin such a process ought to prompt one not to disparage their weaknesses, but to learn from them. Such is the intent of this essay and of the volumes of which it is a part. At its outset, I said that the statesman must play to two different audiences. This essay does no more than provide a few stage directions; it is up to those who occupy positions of responsibility to write the script.

# CHAPTER TEN
# LIMITS AND POSSIBILITIES
## Kenneth W. Thompson

Having considered the influence of political thought and its relationship to contemporary problems, we are left with the issue of the possibilities and limitations of projecting American values abroad. Periodically, the American government and the electorate call on their leaders to tell America's story to the world. The Voice of America, Radio Free Europe and Radio Liberty have all been engaged, in the words of a former Director of the United States Information Agency, in "selling America." Information specialists make up a profession of their own and leave others to debate the relative merits of the "hard" and "soft" sell.

For citizens and general observers and particularly those with a sense of history, the question of projecting American values abroad has broader implications than communications and information specialists suggest. It is a question which preoccupied the founders when they wrote of America as "a beacon on a hill." In the first decades of the republic's history, the new and struggling nation spoke to the world by force of example. It offered mankind an experiment of equality pursued in liberty. The nation had a purpose which kindled hope for those who came to its shores. The concept of a chosen people fired the imagination of European immigrants and inspired the belief that the United States had lessons and experiences to share with others. What the infant nation could not share were values carried abroad by the soldier and the sword. Thus in the debate over the Monroe Doctrine, John Quincy Adams warned that America ought not to pretend it had the means of defending freedom in Europe. It would serve no purpose, for example, to declare support of the Greek independence movement in the 1820s when the only naval force we could muster for action in the Mediterranean was a frigate and a schooner.

Throughout history, the debate over the meaning of American

values for friends abroad has centered on the question of limitations and possibilities. The context of the discussion of limitations has related partly to military power and partly to national purpose, resolve and will. Joined together military preparedness and national purpose constitute the nation's capacity. Ironically, strength in one has not always coincided with strength in the other. In the first decades of its history, the nation was militarily weak although confidence in its purpose was never stronger. For Lincoln as for Jefferson, the cause of liberty would be served only when it spread to foreign soil. In the four decades following World War II, and particularly after America had rearmed, doubts concerning the nation's moral leadership and its sense of purpose were stronger than uncertainty over its military capacity. (The two exceptions were the election campaigns of John F. Kennedy and Ronald Reagan and only the latter pointed exclusively to military weakness.)

A more general limitation which sets constraints not only at election time but throughout the nation's political history results from the nature of the international system. Theorists have described the resistance of sovereign nation states to foreign influences by speaking of the impenetrability of national jurisdictions. Not only does each nation state constitute a closed system to the infusion of alien ideas but the ability of governments to maintain themselves in power depends on unmistakable evidence of the capacity to govern free from outside interference. A legitimate government must demonstrate its capacity for national defense and effective resistance to cultural and political penetration. Totalitarian governments in the nuclear age maintain their power and authority by pointing to an external threat. More fragile governments resist cultural intrusions by claiming absolute authority to shape their educational and social systems. In the 1960s, I asked the young Tanzanian leader, Julius Nyerere, how an outside technical assistance agency could help him strengthen education in the new African nation. Should we make available educational leaders to help at the primary-secondary or the higher education level? Without a moment's hesitation, Nyerere responded: "Help us in higher education. If I fail to provide national educational institutions at the primary-secondary level, my people will reject me and my government and turn us out of power." It remains true that the building of a viable structure of values is a national responsibility in the present international order.

At the same time, the urgent needs of the developing countries surpass available national resources in virtually every one of some one hundred fledgling nation states. As weaker countries looked to Britain, France and Spain for direct help in an earlier era, they have turned to the United States, the Soviet Union, Japan and the more powerful European nations in the present era. If their appeals reflect an anxious mixture of felt need and fear and produce a certain ambivalence verging periodically on schizophrenia, they recur with predictable consistency. If the exigencies of world politics lead them to shift from one source of assistance to another, they demonstrate an unbroken pattern of well-organized calls for help whether put forward in bilateral or multilateral terms.

Moreover, the United States has a long-established tradition of service and assistance that has continued from administration to administration. Educational assistance goes back at least to the turn of the century. Asian students have matriculated in American institutions from the day of the cultural exchanges established following the Boxer Rebellion. American universities have become the centers of world education that prompt some authorities to describe them as "American Heidelbergs;" they have assumed the role played by the great German and European universities in another epoch. The unique strengths of American higher education in fields such as agriculture and medicine have equipped them as worldwide resources in essential spheres of basic human needs. The United States in postwar technical assistance has led from strength in service to the world and its actions have exceeded public understanding of the role it has played.

The public discussion of this role is often obscured by the worldwide controversy over industrialization and freedom. A particularly potent slogan in the developing world is the argument that the new nations reject the pattern of modernization that has occurred in the industrial countries. Neutralist leaders have made political capital by proclaiming they are unwilling to accept the high price of industrialism with its environmental degradation, urban blight and recurrent cycles of inflation and unemployment. It has been fashionable to reject freedom for social welfare. Yet the self-same societies at differing periods in their history have sought the benefits of industrialism and, beneath the surface, the unquenchable search for freedom makes itself manifest in the replacement of thorough-going military regimes by civilian governments. Thus performance and rhetoric follow divergent paths.

Hence a persistent problem in assessing the possibilities of projecting American values abroad is the need to separate words and deeds. The new nations, while protesting against educational institutions which train only elites, seek the most well-trained leaders their resources and those of their friends can produce. For the United States, an especially painful problem is that of expecting gratitude in return for assistance. Yet sovereign governments cannot publicly acknowledge their dependence on others. Even when external aid proves decisive for nations, unstable governments cannot inform their people of the degree of their dependence. As they privately seek help, they publicly proclaim their independence. In the Philippines, Filipinos refer to all outside agencies by their acronyms with one exception. They speak of the World Health

Organization as WHO, of the Food and Agriculture Organization as FAO, and the United Nations Educational, Scientific, and Cultural Organization as UNESCO. However Philippine leaders have been unwilling or unable to call the Agency for International Assistance AID because aid connotes a breach of independence.

In the final analysis, the realities of nationalism require a more subtle and less intrusive viewpoint by those seeking to help. American values to be effective must be seen as reciprocal to the values of friends. The act of helping others must be cast in the language of partnership, not intervention. Americans abroad who would see an effective implementation of their values must live and work within indigenous institutions. The American agronomists and plant pathologists who, beginning in 1943, sought to foster agricultural development in Mexico did so within, not outside, the Mexican Government's Ministry of Agriculture. They established an Office of Special Studies within the Ministry. No longer can American educators in most developing countries serve as Deans or Departmental Chairmen. In the language of public administration, they must be on tap, not on top.

Therefore, patience, forebearance and humility are essential ingredients in any effective program for the sharing of American values in action. It is untrue that American values are irrelevant to the needs of other countries. In the long run, no other set of values has greater relevance, given the nature of man. But the situational context is one of intense national pride in most countries reinforced by the political needs of both leaders and the people. For proud Americans, competing national pride in other lands occasions frustration and resentment. The most urgent requirement is an awareness of how the world is organized and the context in which American values are received. The need for political maturity is the basis of success in projecting American values abroad.

# CHAPTER ONE

[1] Daniel Bell, for instance, believes that the sense of mission has eroded in recent years. "The End of American Exceptionalism," in *The American Commonwealth—1976* edited by Nathan Glazer and Irving Kristol (New York: Basic Books, 1976), 205.

[2] Leon Baritz, *City on a Hill: A History of Ideas and Myths in America* (New York: John Wiley & Sons, Inc., 1964), 100-101.

[3] Ibid., 93-94.

[4] I have found Ernest Lee Tuveson's *Redeemer Nation: The Idea of America's Millenial Role* (Chicago: The University of Chicago Press, 1968) to be extremely helpful, and I must credit Tuveson for much of what I have to say about the importance of religious thinking and the tradition of American fundamentalism.

[5] Baritz, 13.

[6] A few years ago it would have been easy for enlightened, educated people to make light of this tradition. Given the events of the last few years and the impact of groups like the Moral Majority, it is more difficult to be so smug.

[7] Tuveson, ix-x.

[8] Ibid., 23-23, 34.

[9] Ibid., 51.

[10] See, for example, Carl Degler, "The American Past: An Unexpected Obstacle in Foreign Affairs," *The American Scholar* 5 (Spring 1963): 208.

[11] See Felix Gilbert, *To the Farewell Address: Ideas of Early American Foreign Policy* (Princeton, N.J.: Princeton University Press, 1961), esp. chapter III.

[12] In Tuveson, 108-09.

[13] Thomas Bailey, *A Diplomatic History of the American People,* 9th ed., (Englewood Cliffs, N.J.: Prentice-Hall, Inc. 1970) 268.

[14] See Frederick Merk, *Manifest Destiny and Mission in American History* (New York: Vintage Books, 1963).

[15] Ralph Henry Gabriel, *The Course of American Democratic Thought,* 2nd ed., (New York: The Ronald Press, 1965) 385-86.

[16] See Merk, chapter XII.

[17] Address to the Chicago Council on Foreign Relations, March 15, 1976.

[18] Bernard Brodie, *War and Politics* (New York: MacMillan Publishing Co., Inc., 1973), 116.

[19] Gabriel, 25, 372.

[20] E. M. Burns, *The American Idea of Mission: Concepts of National Purpose and Destiny* (New Brunswick, N.J.: Rutgers University Press, 1957), 348-49.

[21] R. E. Osgood, *Ideals and Self-Interest in America's Foreign Relations: The Great Transformation of the Twentieth Century* (Chicago: The University of Chicago Press, 1953), 54.

[22] Kenneth W. Thompson in "Statesmen as Philosophers: Written and Living Theories," *Review of Politics* 20 (October 1958): 441, decries the cloaking of foreign policies in moral purposes as "vulgar and debasing"

but notes that even Winston Churchill, perhaps the twentieth century model of the "realistic" statesman, found it necessary so to cloak his policies.

# CHAPTER TWO

[1] Leo Strauss, *The City and Man* (Chicago: Rand McNally, 1964), 4.
[2] Walter Lippmann, *The Public Philosophy* (London: Hamish Hamilton, 1955), 61.
[3] Hans Morgenthau, *Politics Among Nations,* 5th ed., (New York: Alfred Knopf, 1973), 10.
[4] See Kenneth W. Thompson, *Masters of International Thought* (Baton Rouge, La.: Louisiana State University Press, 1980) for a helpful overview of these and other writers.
[5] Aristotle, *The Nichomachean Ethics,* trans. W. D. Ross (London: Oxford University Press, 1969), 142.
[6] Ibid., 155.
[7] Ibid., 142.
[8] Martin Diamond, "Ethics and Politics: The American Way," in *The Moral Foundations of the American Republic,* ed. Robert H. Horwitz (Charlottesville, Va.: University Press of Virginia, 1977), 45.
[9] Aristotle. 145.
[10] John Courtney Murray, *We Hold These Truths* (New York: Sheed and Ward, 1960), 272.
[11] Blaise Pascal, *Pensees,* trans. W. F. Trotter (New York: Dutton, 1958), 99.
[12] Ibid., 85.
[13] Reinhold Niebuhr, editorial in *Christianity and Crisis,* I, 1 (Feb. 10, 1941), 4.
[14] Ibid.
[15] Murray, 258.
[16] The discussion in this section draws on the distinction between the just war and the crusade made by Roland Bainton and others. In *Christian Attitudes Toward War and Peace* (Nashville: Abingdon Press, 1960), 44, Bainton suggests that the crusade differs from the just war primarily "in its intensely religious quality. The just war, to be sure, was not devoid of religion. . .but it was fought for mundane objectives. . .whereas the Crusade was God's War." The differing aims lead to different attitudes; the attitude of the just warrior is resignation, that of the crusader is zeal to wreak vengence. The differing aims also call forth different use of the available means: limited ends moderate use, whereas crusades issue in indiscriminate violence. LeRoy Walters in "The Just War and the Crusade: Antitheses or Analogies?" *The Monist,* 57 (1973), 584-594 further argues that though medieval theorists did not pose the issue in terms of this antithesis, it is helpful to do so. Nevertheless, the two are not *necessarily* contradictory and the crusade remains a practical possibility in any situation where military force is employed. Realists seek to minimize that possibility

by emphasizing "the national interest," a term devoid of moral appeal. This apparent a-morality, though, often disguises deeper moral concern as their criticisms of U.S. policy in Vietnam suggest.

[17] Herbert Storing, "American Statesmanship: Old and New," *Bureaucrats, Policy Analysts, Statesmen: Who Leads?* ed. Robert Goldwin (Washington, D.C.: American Enterprise Institute, 1980), 88-89.

[18] Henry Kissinger, *White House Years* (Boston: Little, Brown, and Co., 1980), 5.

[19] Alexis de Tocqueville, *Democracy in America,* Vol. II, ed. Phillips Bradley (New York: Vintage Books, 1958), 243-44.

[20] Inis L. Claude, Jr., "The Central Challenge to the United Nations: Weakening the Strong or Strengthening the Weak?" *Harvard International Law Journal,* Vol. 14 (1973), 524.

[21] Tocqueville, 129.

[22] Alexander Hamilton, James Madison, and John Jay, *The Federalist Papers,* ed. Clinton Rossiter (New York: Mentor Books, 1961), 438.

[23] Tocqueville, 131.

[24] Ibid.

[25] Reinhold Niebuhr, *Moral Man and Immoral Society* (New York: Charles Scribner's Sons, 1932), 234.

[26] Reinhold Niebuhr, *Christianity and Crisis,* vol. XXIX, no. 4 (March 17, 1969), 49.

[27] Reinhold Niebuhr, *Man's Nature and His Communities* (New York: Scribner's, 1965), 82.

[28] Harry Clor, "Woodrow Wilson," in *American Political Thought,* ed. Morton J. Frisch and Richard G. Stevens (New York: Scribner's, 1971), 195.

[29] Benjamin Barber, "Command Performance," *Harper's,* Vol. 250, n. 1499, (April, 1975), 56.

# CHAPTER THREE

[1] Joseph Cropsey, "Political Morality and Liberalism," in *Political Philosophy and the Issues of Politics* (University of Chicago Press, Chicago, 1977), 138.

[2] Ibid.

[3] Walter Lippmann, *Essays in the Public Philosophy* (Boston: Little Brown, 1955), 114.

[4] Ibid.

[5] See Martin Diamond, "Ethics and Politics: The American Way," in *The Moral Foundations of the American Republic,* ed. Robert H. Horwitz (Charlottesville: University Press of Virginia, 1979), 43.

[6] Leo Strauss, "Political Philosophy and History," in *What is Political Philosophy?"* (New York: The Free Press, 1959), 70.

[7] Strauss, 43.

[8] Ibid.

[9] Ibid., 103.

[10] Leo Strauss, *Natural Right and History* (Chicago: University of Chicago Press, 1953), 193.

[11] In Dante Germino, *Beyond Ideology: The Revival of Political Theory* (New York: Harper and Row, 1967), 143.

[12] Martin Diamond, 61.

[13] Leo Strauss, "What is Political Philosophy?" in *What is Political Philosophy?* (New York: The Free Press, 1959), 46.

[14] Ibid., 42.

[15] See Hannah Arendt, "Tradition and the Modern Age," in *Between Past and Future: Eight Essays in Political Thought* (New York: Viking, 1961).

[16] Germino, 141.

[17] Quoted in Kenneth W. Thompson, *Morality and Foreign Policy* (Baton Rouge: Louisiana State University Press, 1980), 157.

[18] Quoted in Eric Voegelin, *The New Science of Politics* (Chicago: University of Chicago Press, 1952), 174.

[19] Ibid., 175.

[20] Cropsey, 138.

[21] Diamond, 40.

[22] Voegelin, 175.

[23] Alexis de Tocqueville, *The Ancient Regime and the French Revolution,* trans. Stuart Gilbert (Garden City, New York: Doubleday, 1955), 146-47.

[24] Michael Walzer, *Radical Principles: Reflections of an Unreconstructed Democrat* (New York: Basic Books, 1980), 45.

[25] Robert Heilbroner, "What is Socialiam?" *Dissent,* Summer 1978, 42.

[26] Herbert Storing, "Bureaucracy and Statesmanship," *Bureaucrats, Policy Analysts and Statesmen,* ed. Robert Goldwin (Washington, D.C.: American Enterprise Institute, 1979), 64.

[27] Strauss, *What is Political Philosophy?,* 92.

[28] George Will, *The Pursuit of Happiness and Other Sobering Thoughts* (New York: Harper Colophon, 1978), 206.

[29] Alexis de Tocqueville, *Democracy in America,* ed. Phillips Bradley, 2 Vols. (New York: Random House, 1945), 42, Vol. II.

[30] Ibid.

[31] Thompson, 141.

# CHAPTER FOUR

[1] "The great and chief end therefore, of Mens uniting into Commonwealths, and putting themselves under Government, is the Preservation of their Property." Locke, 395. All quotes from *Two Treatises* are taken from the Mentor edition: John Locke, *Two Treatises of Government: A Critical Edition with an Introduction and Apparatus Criticus* by Peter Laslett, New American Library, New York, 1963.

[2] Locke, 367.

[3] It is often observed that the wording of the Declaration of In-

dependence, "life, liberty, and the pursuit of happiness", is a significant alteration of Locke's formulation of "life, liberty, and estate." In fact "pursuit of happiness" may come closer to expressing Locke's understanding of property than the established material possessions that "estate" implies. Since the justification for private property is individual labor, Lockean property is a kind of human activity that has a broad motivation and is clearly expressed in the phrase "pursuit of happiness."

⁴ Locke, 367.
⁵ Ibid., 397.
⁶ Ibid., 407.
⁷ Ibid., 448.
⁸ Ibid., 419.
"If therefore the Executive, who has the power of Convoking the Legislative, observing rather the true proportion, than fashion of Representation, regulates, not by old custom, but true reason, the number of Members, in all places, that have a right to be distinctly represented, which no part of the People however incorporated can pretend to, but in proportion to the assistance, which it affords to the publick, it cannot be judg'd to have set up a new Legislative, but to have restored the old and true one."
⁹ Ibid., 425.
¹⁰ Ibid., 422.
¹¹ Ibid., 372.
¹² Ibid., 422.

# CHAPTER FIVE

¹ Hans J. Morgenthau, *Politics Among Nations: The Struggle for Power and Peace,* Fifth Ed. Rev. (New York: Alfred A. Knopf, 1978), 274.
² Christopher Dawson, *The Making of Europe,* (New York: Meridian Books, 1956), 169-238.
³ See the writings of Niebuhr, especially *The Structure of Nations and Empires, Moral Man and Immoral Society,* and *The Irony of American History.*

# CHAPTER SIX

¹ *Discorsi* III, 1 and *Istorie Fiorentine,* V, 1 in A. Panella, ed., *Niccolo Machiavelli: Opere* (2 vols., Rizzoli, 1939), II, 280 and I, 348.
² *Discorsi,* I, 9 in Panella, op. cit., II 131-32. Hereinafter cited as *Opere.*
³ Il principe, ch. 18. 18 in *Opere,* II, 66.
⁴ Letter to Soderini of January, 1513 in *Opere,* II, 780.

⁵ *History of Florence* (F. Gilbert, ed., New York, Harper and Row, 1960) 165.

⁶ Sheldon S. Wolin, *Politics and Vision* (Boston, 1960), 220-31.

⁷ Ibid., 224.

⁸ Ibid., 230.

⁹ Ibid., 221.

¹⁰ Ibid., 230.

¹¹ Ibid., 220. It is all the more puzzling that Wolin should not have seen the implications of his comments on Machiavelli, for he has written eloquently of the need for humanistic vision in politics and of the unacceptability of a political science preoccupied with "technique."

# CHAPTER NINE

¹ Quoted in Arnold Wolfers and Laurence W. Martin, eds., *The Anglo-American Tradition in Foreign Affairs: Readings From Thomas More to Woodrow Wilson* (New York: Yale University Press, 1956), 147, 149.

² "Does It Matter Whether America Matters?" *New Republic* 181 (September 22, 1979):18.

³ U.S., President, *Public Papers of the Presidents of the United States* (Washington, D.C.: Office of the *Federal Register,* National Archives and Records Service, 1953-    ), Jimmy Carter, 1977, 958.

⁴ Ibid., Richard M. Nixon, 1970, 119.

⁵ W. W. Rostow, *The United States in the World Arena: An Essay in Recent History* (New York: Harper and Row, 1960; reprint ed., New York: Simon and Schuster, 1969), 544.

⁶ Nixon, *Public Papers,* 1970, 118-119.

⁷ Ibid., 1969, 905-906.

⁸ Ibid., 1970, 117-118.

⁹ Ibid., 1972, 211.

¹⁰ Ibid., 1970, 179. See also the discussion of U.S. policy toward China in Nixon, *Public Papers,* 1973, 352.

¹¹ Ibid., 1973, 404.

¹² *Time* 99 (January 3, 1972):15.

¹³ Nixon, *Public Papers,* 1971, 238; 1972, 237; 1973, 425.

¹⁴ Ibid., 1971, 889.

¹⁵ Jimmy Carter, *Why Not the Best? Why One Man Is Optimistic About America's Third Century* (Nashville: Broadman Press, 1975), 123.

¹⁶ These three examples of Carter's campaign rhetoric in 1975 and 1976 are taken from the selections from his speeches in Jimmy Carter, *A Government as Good as Its People* (New York: Simon and Schuster, 1977), 71-72, 69, 169.

¹⁷ Carter, *Public Papers,* 1979, 158.

¹⁸ Ibid., 1977, 956.

¹⁹ Ibid., 1978, 96.

²⁰ Ibid., 1977, 961.

[21] Ibid., 3.

[22] Ibid., 1978, 1053.

[23] Ibid., 1055.

[24] Ibid., 1977, 3, 4, 959.

[25] U.S., President, *Weekly Compilation of Presidential Documents* 16 (January-March 1980), 163; Carter *Public Papers,* 1979, 720.

[26] Carter, *A Government as Good as Its People,* 116.

[27] Carter, *Public Papers,* 1977, 3.

[28] Ibid., 1979, 157.

[29] The selection from the Inaugural Address is printed in Carter, *Public Papers,* 1977, 2; that from the 1981 State of the Union Address in U.S., Congress, Senate, 97th Cong., 1st sess., 19 January 1981, *Congressional Record* 127:243; and that from the Farewell Address in Department of State *Bulletin* 81 (February, 1981), 23.

[30] Carter, *Public Papers,* 1977, 3.

[31] Department of State *Bulletin* 81 (February 1981), 23.

[32] Carter *Public Papers,* 1977, 2; 1979, 161.

[33] Ibid., 1978, 97.

[34] *Weekly Compilation of Presidential Documents* 16 (October-December 1980), 2340; Carter, *Public Papers,* 1977, 2. The president's personal commitment to a stand on morality should not be taken as a sign that this was a personal prediliction, unshared by others in the administration. For the belief of Vice President Walter Mondale, presidential press secretary and confidant Jody Powell, and other Carter subordinates in the need for "a convergence of policy and values. . . .if we're going to feel good about our society," see Elizabeth Drew, "Human Rights," *The New Yorker,* 18 July 1977, 36-62.

[35] Carter, *Public Papers,* 1977, 955.

[36] Ibid., 1978, 95; 1977, 956.

[37] Ibid., 1979, 636-637.

[38] Ibid., 95.

[39] Ibid., 531, 532.

[40] The Kissinger quote is from his October 8, 1973 address, "Moral Purposes and Policy Choices," delivered to the third Pacem in Terris Conference and reprinted in the Department of State *Bulletin* 69 (October, 29, 1973):525-531; the Carter quote, from his Inaugural Address, Carter *Public Papers,* 1977, 2.

[41] This argument is vigorously presented in Eugene David Weinstein, "The Ignoble Lie—National Interest Ideology in American Civilization" (Ph.D. dissertation, University of Minnesota, 1967).